THIS IS NUMBER ONE HUNDRED
AND TWENTY-SEVEN IN THE
SECOND NUMBERED SERIES OF THE
MIEGUNYAH VOLUMES
MADE POSSIBLE BY THE
MIEGUNYAH FUND
ESTABLISHED BY BEQUESTS
UNDER THE WILLS OF
SIR RUSSELL AND LADY GRIMWADE.

'MIEGUNYAH' WAS THE HOME OF
MAB AND RUSSELL GRIMWADE
FROM 1911 TO 1955.

HOLLY KERR FORSYTH

The GARDENER'S
Book of Days

THE
MIEGUNYAH
PRESS

THE MIEGUNYAH PRESS
An imprint of Melbourne University Publishing Limited
187 Grattan Street, Carlton, Victoria 3053, Australia
mup-info@unimelb.edu.au
www.mup.com.au

First published 2010
Text and photography © Holly Kerr Forsyth, 2010
www.theconstantgardener.com.au
Design and typography © Melbourne University Publishing
Limited, 2010

Edited by Penny Mansley
Image management by Dave Bishop, Sun Studios
Designed by Pfisterer + Freeman
Typeset by Pfisterer + Freeman
Printed and bound in Malaysia for Imago

National Library of Australia Cataloguing-in-Publication entry

Forsyth, Holly Kerr
The gardener's book of days/Holly Kerr Forsyth.
ISBN 9780522856729 (pbk.)
Includes index.
Gardening—Australia.
635.0994

Contents

Welcome

Have you ever been struck by the serendipity of life, or thought about just how clever nature is when left well alone? Have you been moved to tears when struck by an overwhelming sense of place in a beautiful location, or mused over the advice that garlic should be planted on shortest day of the year and harvested on its longest?

I have had enormous fun writing this book, discovering all sorts of facts to provide amusement and fascination for every day of the year. There is the practical: when do you plant your beetroot, when should you be alert for citrus leaf miner, and how do make the most of your winter-laden lemon trees? There is the romantic: daffodils should be picked on Father's Day and olives on Mother's Day. There is the historic: do you know in which garden the 25-year-old Princess Elizabeth was sitting when told that her half-sister Mary had died, and that she was to be crowned Queen of England? Then there is the kind of trivia treasured by garden lovers everywhere: when was the great rosarian Graham Stuart Thomas born and who were the women after whom the Australian rose breeder, Alister Clark, named his roses? How did the 'Granny Smith' apple come about?

The Gardener's Book of Days notes that you should plant your sweet peas by St Patrick's Day, fertilise camellias when the footie season starts and gather up your pumpkins when the frost kills the foliage. It provides advice on achieving the best results from your orchids and on pruning your fuchsias. It reminds you when to divide plants and when to refresh your potting mix. It is a light-hearted, fact-packed book to dip into, to take up when you have just five minutes to spare, or to read daily to remind yourself of what to do when.

I hope you enjoy it.

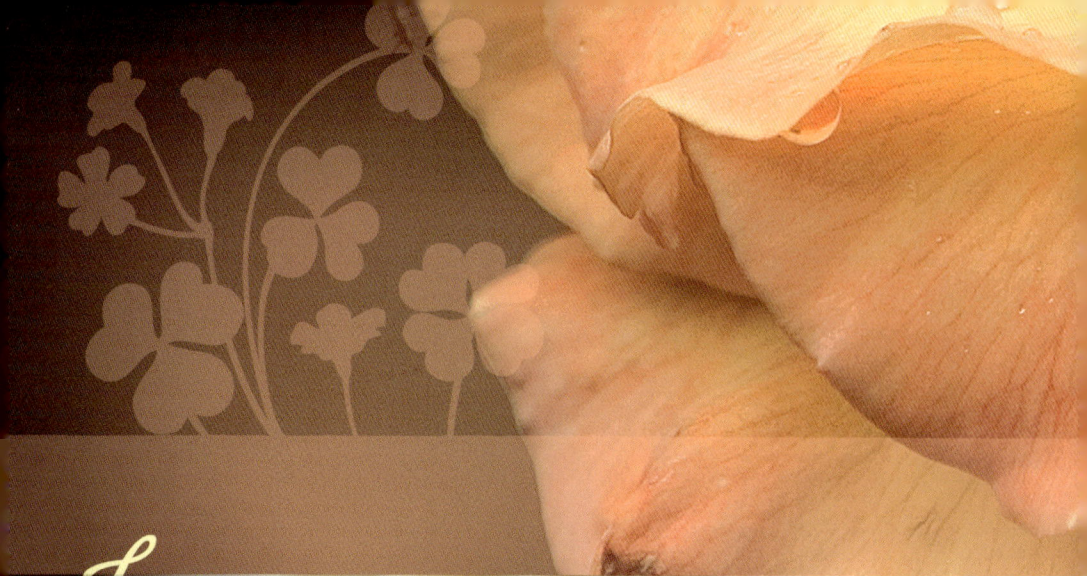

January

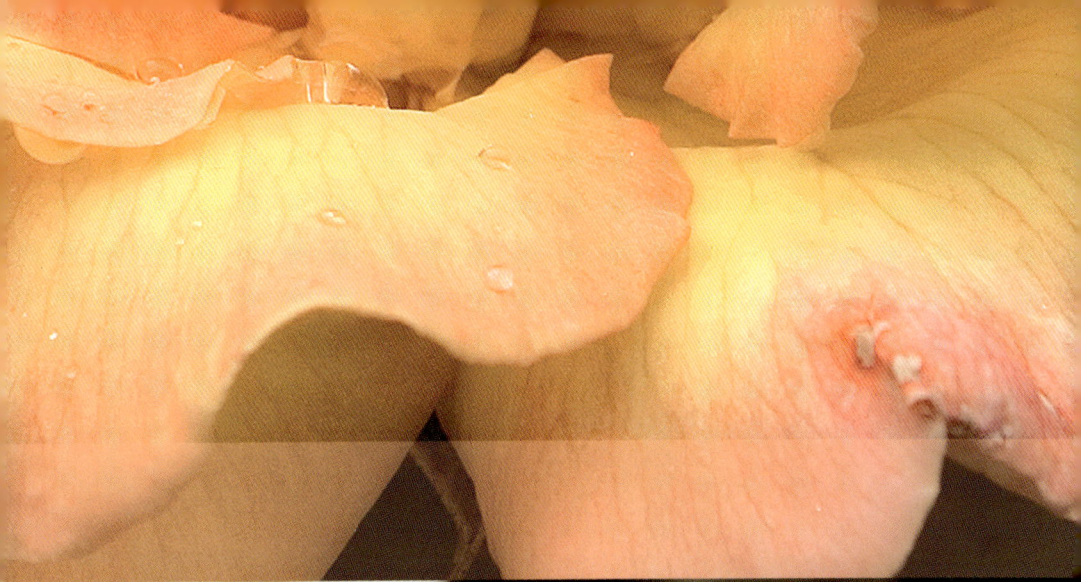

1 January

A new year …

It's the beginning of a new year, and, of course, the starting point for all sorts of good intentions. Along with taking more exercise and giving up unhealthy foods, we all intend to be better gardeners: to grow more vegetables, dead-head and weed regularly, water wisely, and, most importantly, mulch heavily. In January, when the days may be too hot to tempt you into the garden at any time but early morning, or in the balmy evenings, good garden-keeping reaps rewards.

Today, however, you deserve a rest: this is a chance to put your feet up and indulge in some holiday reading with the sounds of the cricket to keep you company, having done nothing more strenuous than picking the sky-blue flowers of the borage in your herb garden to add to ice cubes for your mint tea.

New Year's Day—time to relax!

2 January

Harold Hillier

The English arborist Harold Hillier was born on this day in 1905. His famous family nursery, located at Romsey in the English county of Hampshire, sponsored plant hunters such as Ernest 'Chinese' Wilson, who explored the mountains of China to bring the Western world some of its most loved species. Today, the Sir Harold Hillier Gardens attract thousands of visitors annually. And the *Hillier Manual of Trees and Shrubs* is still in publication, after many editions; it's a must-have for every gardener, no matter in which part of the world you garden.

3 January

Holiday ready

It's time to get your garden 'holiday ready'. If you have ever returned from a summer holiday to find your green oasis gasping for water—or, worse, fatally scorched by the January heat—the experience may have remained indelibly printed on your mind. As you struggled to revive it, or were forced to replant it, one of your new year's resolutions may have been to prepare your garden in plenty of time for future hot summers. So, if you are planning to head off on holiday during the month, leaving your garden to cope alone, or if you simply find the weather too hot to spend much time outdoors, think about strategies for saving your garden from the summer heat.

When preparing your plants for a heatwave, your first task will be to clear the garden of weeds, as they'll be greedy for precious nutrients and moisture. Then, cut plants back—leaving the prunings on the ground to return to the soil—and provide a light feed of a complete food like Dynamic Lifter. Soak well (of course, only as permitted) and then—and this is the key—apply a really thick layer of your preferred mulch. (A mulch of 7.5 centimetres' depth can save water use by some 30 per cent.) My favourite mulch is spoiled lucerne, which can be bought in bales from your local cooperative, or chopped and conveniently packed into manageable bags from your local nursery. There are many organic wetting agents you can add to your soil, also, to help in conserving moisture.

The Granny Smith apple

4 January

A fresh apple

The 'Granny Smith' apple was 'born' in Australia, and was named after Maria Anne Smith (nee Sherwood), who was born in England in 1799, and was baptised on this day in 1800. The daughter of a farm labourer, she married Thomas Smith in 1819. They migrated to Sydney on the *Lady Nugent*, in 1838. In the mid 1850s, Thomas established an orchard of about 10 hectares on the edge of the Field of Mars Common, now Eastwood; Maria developed the apple that was eventually named after her from a seedling grown on the property.

Maria died on 9 March 1870 at Ryde. The apple was not a commercial variety during her lifetime, but its cultivation was sustained by local orchardists. By the end of the nineteenth century, 'Granny Smith's Apples' were winning prizes in competition cooking-apple classes, and the seedlings were planted on a large scale at the Government Experimental Station at Bathurst. In 1895, the variety was listed by the Department of Agriculture as suitable for export; thus began its long and successful commercial life.

Pots

Pots: terracotta, ceramic, wooden and plastic. They are the saviours of all who garden in small spaces. The range of receptacles in which you can grow plants is limited only by your imagination: I have seen petunias growing in old work boots, and china teapots, iron buckets and watering cans (all with drainage holes drilled in the base) planted up with different species. Plants in pots can need a little more attention, however, than those that can get their roots down into deep, well-mulched soil. For a start, potted plants dry out more quickly, and their soil needs replacing regularly.

Paint the inside of terracotta pots with a sealer to prevent moisture loss, and always mulch pot plants well. And, when planting bulbs in pots, place some old pantyhose in the base (before you add the potting mix) to prevent the slaters that love to hide under pots from crawling up through the soil to feast on your bulbs.

Clay pots in a garden in Shiraz, Iran

If you are to be away on holidays, move pots into a cool area, in a spot where they will catch any rain that falls. Position them together, on a pile of newspaper that has been soaked well in water. Or, stand them on saucers filled with water (though don't make this normal practice when you're at home—plants left standing in moisture in this way will not have the necessary drainage).

6 January

Seeds in space

As part of an experiment designed to assist in the preservation of threatened species, seeds of several native Australian plants have been transported into space. In May 2008, NASA astronaut Dr Gregory Chamitoff took seeds of the New South Wales waratah (*Telopea speciosissima*), the golden wattle (*Acacia pycnantha*) and the Wollemi pine (*Wollemia nobilis*) on a mission to the International Space Station. The experiment was initiated by Sydney's Royal Botanic Gardens Trust to ascertain whether Australian seeds, among the hardiest in the botanical world, could provide oxygen on the moon. It was also hoped that the exercise would highlight the importance of seed-banking in ensuring the survival of species under threat due to global warming and other changes in habitat.

7 January

Water tanks

In a perfect example of the saying 'Everything old is new again', many households have installed water tanks. As they now come in an almost endless variety of shapes and sizes, from slim and tall to short and fat, made from corrugated iron, from plastic or from rubber bladders that can slide under a house, or under a verandah, there is, probably, a water tank to suit every property. While water restrictions introduced over the past decade have shown us that we can, indeed, use less water on our gardens, most of us don't want to see rain, when it does fall, wash into gutters and stormwater drains.

A 100 000-litre underground domestic water-tank at Susan and Graeme Jack's garden, Jack's Ridge, is cleverly hidden beneath a beautiful parterre of lavender and buxus.

8 January

Clean Up Australia

Clean Up Australia Day was started by property developer and yachtsman Ian Kiernan on this day in 1989, with the intention of simply making a difference in his own backyard: Sydney Harbour. Two decades later, hundreds of thousands of Australians take part in cleaning up their local community by collecting and removing rubbish on Clean Up Australia Day, now held annually, often on the first Sunday in March.

The Clean Up Australia website (www.cleanup.org.au) gives some frightening statistics about how much rubbish we produce; for example, each year, an estimated 7 billion cigarette butts end up in Australian waterways, streets and parklands, and 80 million plastic bags are discarded. Over the past two decades, Clean Up Australia Day participants have collected over 200 000 tonnes of rubbish—that's 4.7 million household wheelie bins. It's easy to get involved: once you have selected your site—which could be a local park, part of the bush, a river, a waterway—you can register with Clean Up Australia via the website. You will then receive a kit containing refuse bags, gloves and posters, and a 'site guide' outlining everything you need to know about cleaning up your chosen area. And let your local council know: they will often arrange to remove your bags of collected refuse.

9 January

Waterlilies

The waterlily, or lotus (*Nymphaea* spp.), is named for the nymphs in Greek mythology. Revered throughout history and around the world, from the kings and queens of Ancient Egypt to the impressionist painters of the twentieth century, the waterlily has long been central to legend, literature and landscape. No plant epitomises the water garden better than the waterlily. There are about fifty species of waterlily, which come from eight genera of water plants in the Nymphaeceae family. Waterlilies can be both evergreen and deciduous; some are frost-hardy, while others are tropical; some are scented, and most flower for months, from spring, through summer, and into early autumn, with blooms held above rounded leaves that float on the surface of the water. The flowers are often white or cream, but also come in just about every other colour, from blue and purple to pink, red, yellow and orange. Most turn their faces to the sun, although some are night-blooming.

Waterlilies provide shade for fish and other water-dwelling creatures, and are among the beneficial plants essential for oxygenating the water and crowding out non-beneficial algae, which take up sunlight and nutrients. They can be bought in containers, or by mail order, bare-rooted. If you receive plants by mail order, submerge the roots for a day in a tub of water: don't allow them to dry out before planting. Try planting waterlilies in a variety of receptacles—a bowl, barrel, pond or dam. Put some stones at the bottom of a hessian-lined basket or a plastic pot, which will help to keep it stable on the base of your water feature. Then fill it with an aquatic mix or compost-rich soil and plant the waterlily in this. Firm the soil down well, as, once

Summer in Centennial Park, Sydney, and the waterlilies bloom

submerged, air will be dispelled from the container, and the soil level will drop. Cover the top with gravel so that the soil does not wash away. Place the basket or pot onto bricks in your water feature, at a height to allow the leaves to float on the water surface, or, if the plant is leafless, to bring it just below the surface. Gradually remove the bricks as the plant sends out roots towards the bottom of the water feature, anchoring the pot in place.

All water plants are greedy, so feed them with a slow-release fertiliser, or, each autumn, jam a fertiliser tablet into the soil in the pot. Propagate by separating plants when flowering is finished. Waterlilies can be susceptible to aphids, but fish or goldfish will usually keep such pests at bay. Repot, after flowering, every few years.

10 January

Unique places

January and February, when the weather can be a little more reliable, are the perfect months to walk, and climb, in the high country of Tasmania. In the Great Western Tiers, which run from the north to the south of the state, like a central spine, are pristine isolated meadows, species of plants endemic

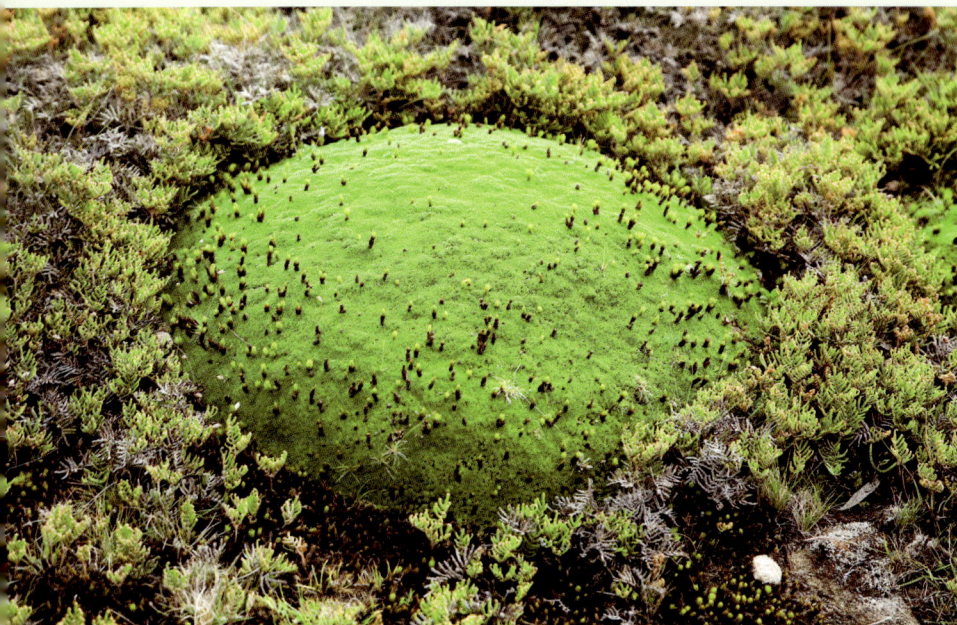

Cushion plants in an alpine meadow beneath Mother Cumming's Peak, Tasmania

to tiny sections of the world, and stunning alpine lakes. Among the mosses that thrive there, with little human disturbance, are the strange and beautiful cushion plants (*Chionohebe ciliolata*), with tiny ovate leaves that range in colour from deep green to brilliant lime green: their hue is determined by the amount of light they receive. Sweet white five-petalled flowers nestle on these plump cushions.

11 January

Fungi

The largest and oldest living being is thought to be an underground colony of toadstools that covers 9 square kilometres in Oregon in the United States: it is believed to be 8000 years old.

Many of us think of fungi as poisonous, our imaginations fed by those brightly coloured, red-and-white spotted toadstools (*Amanita muscaria*) of our childhood fairytales. But fungi are vital to the ecosystem, playing an essential part in recycling and in soil health. The study of fungi is called 'mycology', and, for those interested in the plants, the British Mycological Society (www.britmycolsoc.org.uk) was founded in 1896 and has over 1000 members worldwide. A little later, in 1995, the Australasian Mycological Society (http://bugs.bio.usyd.edu.au/AustMycolSoc/Home/ams.html) was founded, to further communication about, research into and preservation of fungi.

12 January

Salvias

Now is the time to cut back and thin out your salvias. While these members of the mint family can be a garden salvation in the hot months, they can also be a little thuggish, often swamping more gentle treasures. After the first flush of flowers, therefore, reduce growth that has flowered, and is becoming 'leggy', by about three-quarters. Pull out some runners that may appear rampant.

13 January

Garden writing

It is endlessly fascinating to dip into old texts. Writers over the centuries have been remarkably prescient on garden-making, style and design. In *La Theorie et la Pratique du Jardinage* (*The Theory and Practice of Gardening*), published in 1712, the French architect and garden designer Jean-Baptiste Alexandre Le Blond wrote that there are 'four fundamental maxims' that should be observed in garden design:

> Art must give place to nature.
> Gardens should not be made dull and gloomy,
>   by clouding them with thickets and too much cover.
> Gardens should not lay too open,
>   so that it is needless to go into them.
> A garden should always look bigger than it really is.

Not much has changed in landscape theory, more than four centuries later.

14 January

Port Arthur

The penal settlement of Port Arthur, on the Tasman Peninsula, was established in 1830, for transported convicts who had re-offended after their arrival in the colonies. By 1854, Port Arthur had become a town of 2000 people, with substantial buildings and gardens. The officers, many of whom were members of the influential Royal Society of Tasmania, enjoyed gardens around their houses, created with convict labour.

Today, Port Arthur is a beautiful and fascinating place to visit. Recent conservation work, using diaries, journals, sketches and paintings, has resulted in the restoration of some of the major ruins, including Government Cottage, which was used for guests of the governor and visiting dignitaries. The path leading to the cottage is lined with plants that were newly fashionable at the time: a pergola is covered in *Rosa multiflora*, and a path beneath is lined with *Acanthus mollis*, foxgloves and roses. There is the moss rose 'William Lobb', which was bred in 1855; the damask rose 'Mme Hardy' of 1832; *R. multiflora* var. *carnea* of 1804 and the heavily scented Bourbon rose 'Mme Isaac Pereire'. Flower beds surround the Accountant's House and the Junior Medical Officer's House, with their convict-hewn sandstone fence posts and gutter edgings. Next door, at the Catholic Chaplain's House, the garden is planted with fuchsias, the rose 'Veilchenblau' and buddleia, as well as flax plants, a reminder of early attempts to establish a flax industry in the area.

15 January

Ripening rosellas

Growing up in sub-tropical Queensland, I loved the tangy-sweet flavour of the rosella jam that was made each summer by an elderly neighbour. The rosella is, in fact, the immature pod that forms on the yellow-flowering *Hibiscus sabdariffa*, a member of the Malvaceae family, from which many edible plants derive. Although the jam is a little tedious to make, it is worth the effort, as it can be enjoyed on toast, with cheese or with savoury dishes. You can also use it as a demi-glaze, add it to fried onions to make an onion jam, or make it into a rich, slightly sweet sauce for meats. It is particularly delicious with game meats such as kangaroo.

To preserve the jam, you will need sterilised jars: wash your jars and lids in hot water. Place in a preheated 100°C oven for 10–15 minutes, or until dry. Fill immediately with the warm jam.

If it's summer, the rosellas are ripening, ready for cooking into jam.

Rosella jam

1 kg rosellas, chopped

1 kg caster sugar

1 teaspoon ground cinnamon

1 teaspoon ground allspice

3 cloves (remove after cooking), or 1 teaspoon ground cloves

zest and juice 7 lemons or limes

1 cup water

Mix all ingredients together and leave to macerate for 1 hour in a covered bowl. Tip into a heavy-bottomed saucepan and simmer for 10 minutes, or until all sugar has dissolved. Boil rapidly for a further 2–3 hours, or until jam starts to darken. Remove from heat, allow to cool slightly, and (very carefully, as it will still be hot enough to burn) strain into a bowl through a fine sieve or muslin cloth. Remove all the seeds, but, unless you want it to be jelly-like, add back some of the pulp, which is delicious. Pour into warm, sterilised jars. Makes 1 litre.

16 January

The firewheel tree

One of the most easy-going Australian native trees is the spectacular Queensland firewheel (*Stenocarpus sinuatus*), a rainforest tree from the north-east of the country. A member of the Proteaceae family, from a genus of about thirty species, seven of which are native to Australia, the firewheel tree bears deep-green, glossy, leathery leaves and flamboyant red to orange flowers— that are arranged like a wheel—in summer and into autumn. The native birds love them. Despite its origins, the firewheel tree is happy in cooler climates; it likes rich, well-drained, loamy soil.

17 January

Palladio

The work of Andrea Palladio, born in Padua, northern Italy, on 30 November 1508, remains among the most important in the history of architecture. He left a legacy of magnificent municipal buildings, churches and grand town and country residences, in and around the city of Vicenza; restrained gardens of evergreens, stone and water were established in perfect counterpoint to his exquisitely proportioned buildings, with their clean lines and pure symmetry. Palladio's work has influenced architecture the world over, copied by Lord Burlington in England in the eighteenth century and by Thomas Jefferson for his beloved home, Monticello, and for the University of Virginia at Charlottesville.

The spring flowering, once-only, rambling rose 'Dorothy Perkins' was bred in 1901 in the United States. To achieve a stunning specimen like this grafted standard, you should prune in summer, as soon as the blooms fade.

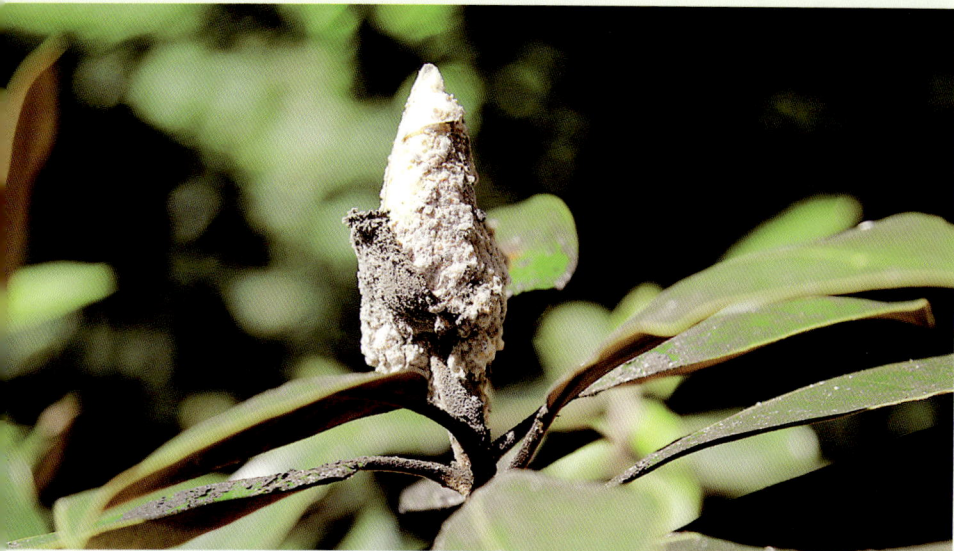

Hot and humid conditions encourage infestations of mealy bug.

19 January

Pests and diseases

Summer heat, together with rain, provides the perfect environment for a plethora of pests. Happily, there is now a range of non-toxic products that can prevent any pest from becoming an infestation, particularly if you combat it early, at the beginning of its life cycle, and before it makes itself completely at home.

It is mealy bug time, and, if not addressed early, this common sap-sucking pest will cover, and smother, a wide range of plants. Mealy bugs are small, white or grey oval insects, and they usually have a short waxy fringe around their bodies. They love humid, sheltered areas in the middle of hedges, or on plants growing on balconies, where air circulation is less than perfect. They feed on all the growing parts of a plant, and exude a sugary substance which ants love, and on which an unsightly sooty mould grows, which will clog the pores of the plant. So you must break the cycle. Prevent their becoming a problem with regular sprays of eco-oil, starting at the beginning of summer. If just a few bugs appear, you can remove them with a cotton bud dipped in methylated spirits, but if the problem becomes severe before you notice it, treat with a low-toxic, systemic spray such as Confidor; in the worst cases you may need to drench the soil with a Confidor solution.

White louse, or wax scale, appears on plants with poor health or growing in low-light environments with insufficient circulation, such as in pots on verandahs. Large infestations have the appearance of white powder, which often covers stems and branches, weakening the plant and causing dieback. The lice also secrete a sugar substance, or honeydew, which attracts ants and aphids, and forms a sooty mould over the leaves, which, apart from looking unsightly, can reduce photosynthesis. Scrape off the severe infestations with a brush, or spray with eco-oil or Confidor, and improve the health of the plants by providing better conditions.

White threads over plants indicate the presence of powdery mildew, which is often worse in humid climates. Spray infected plants weekly with a solution of one part full-cream milk to nine parts water, or with a seaweed fertiliser, or use any of the prepared copper-based products available. Along with black spot on roses, the mildew can also be countered with an organic spray of 3 teaspoons of bicarbonate of soda and 2.5 tablespoons of PestOil in 4.5 litres of water. Spray, covering the entire plant, three times in a fortnight, and then weekly.

It is also time for hibiscus beetles, which, again, can be controlled with eco-oil or Confidor spray. Or, place containers of soapy water near the affected plant, or hang on it cut-outs smeared with Vaseline, to send these small black beetles to a sticky end.

Hot and dry weather can bring ants—often a sign that your plant is gasping for water. Add a wetting agent to your watering can, mulch garden beds and insert water-holding crystals into pots. Barriers such as Tanglefoot, applied around the base of pots, also deter ants.

20 January

Alister Clark

The rosarian Alister Clark died on this day in 1949. He is best remembered for the glorious roses he developed at his home Glenara, near Bulla, today just north of Melbourne's Tullamarine Airport. He was educated in Australia and England, was a polo player, a racing man and a photographer, and

Above: The Alister Clark Memorial Garden
Previous pages: The Alister Clark rose 'Lady Huntingfield'

bred daffodils as well as roses. He named many of his roses after female friends of the family; several were leaders in their fields. 'Amy Johnson', bred in 1931, was named after the aviator, while 'Cicily Lascelles' was named for the golfer. The gorgeous apricot-pink remontant climbing rose 'Lorraine Lee', a second-generation hybrid from *Rosa gigantea*, bred in 1924, is named after a relative. The red-flowering 'Nancy Hayward', named after a rose lover from Adelaide, blooms in winter, while the glorious deep-pink 'Mrs Fred Danks' was named for one of Clark's gardening colleagues.

21 January

Apricots

Each January, a friend who lives a few hours south of Sydney sends us bags of apricots that she picks from 50-year-old trees that she inherited when she bought her property. I am the delighted recipient of such a large quantity, as I bake them, to use in a variety of ways. I halve them, removing the stones, place them on a baking tray, drizzle over balsamic vinegar and brown sugar, and top them with a few dabs of butter. Then I bake them in a very low oven

(100°C) for between two and three hours. If I want additional pizzaz, before baking I add a sprinkling of cinnamon, allspice and crushed cardamom, and even pour over the juice of a couple of oranges. I use these tangy-sweet apricots in shortcake, and with thick plain yoghurt. I serve them, also, with my Persian roast chicken.

Almond blossom spills over a mudbrick wall in Iran

Persian roast chicken with fragrant couscous

FOR THE CHICKEN

6 coriander seeds, crushed, or 3 teaspoons ground coriander

1 teaspoon ground cardamom

1 star anise (whole)

3 teaspoons cumin seeds

garlic (to taste), crushed

30 g butter

1 tablespoon olive oil

1 tablespoon sesame oil

salt and freshly ground pepper

6 chicken half-breasts, wing and skin attached
   (most butchers call this cut 'chicken supreme')

Preheat oven to 180°C. Fry garlic, spices and seasoning in butter and oils, and paste the mix over skin of chicken. Place chicken pieces side by side in a roasting tray, and cook for 1 hour. Turn oven to grill and brown chicken skin for about 10 minutes. Remove from oven and keep warm.

FOR THE FRAGRANT COUSCOUS
50 g raisins
250 ml orange juice
juice 1 lime (optional)
1 onion
garlic (to taste), crushed
1 tablespoon olive oil
1 teaspoon cinnamon
250 g couscous, cooked in
    150 ml chicken stock
100 g pistachios
½ cup coriander, mint or
    flat-leaved parsley, chopped

Soak raisins in juice. Sauté onion and garlic in olive oil, then add cinnamon. Stir in couscous; add raisin mixture and stir over a low heat for several minutes. Remove from heat, and mix in pistachios and chopped herbs. Serve in a shallow dish with the chicken pieces placed on top, and with baked apricots and a sambal of plain yoghurt. Serves six.

22 January

Queen Victoria

Queen Victoria died on this day, on the Isle of Wight, in 1901. She had reigned over the United Kingdom and the British Empire from 1837; at sixty-four years, this remains the longest reign in British history. One of her favourite flowers was the English primrose (*Primula vulgaris*), early to flower in spring and a symbol of British hardiness in the face of adversity. When Prime Minister Benjamin Disraeli died, on 19 April 1881, Victoria sent wreaths of primroses to be placed on his coffin. England's Primrose Day sprang from this gesture.

23 January

Historic houses

According to *The Sydney Monitor* published on this day in 1836, Alexander Macleay 'gave a splendid fete at his villa at Elizabeth Bay. It was attended by the officers of HMS *Beagle* and *Zebra*, many of the military and civil officers and a number of inhabitants'. Macleay had arrived with his wife and six of his children, in January 1826, to take up the post of colonial secretary under New South Wales's Governor Darling. This was one of many receptions held in his garden at Elizabeth Bay House, on the shores of Sydney Harbour. Noted as the most beautiful in the colony, the garden, covering 2.2 hectares, and set within a land grant of some 25 hectares, took twenty men a full ten years to create. It became the repository for species from around the globe, including from China, from where Macleay imported wisteria. Elizabeth Bay House was a rendezvous for the colony's scientific elite, while the garden, described by Joseph Hooker as a 'botanists' paradise', provided a fitting location for the family to display its intellectual and aesthetic strengths. The house is now managed by the Historic Houses Trust (www.hht.net.au), which is charged with preserving, and opening to the public, several important historic properties in New South Wales.

24 January

Edith Wharton

The writer Edith Wharton was born on this day in 1862. Aunt of the landscape architect Beatrix Jones Farrand, Wharton was herself a great gardener: her aesthetic was influenced by years of travel in Italy, and in 1904 she published *Italian Villas and Their Gardens*. She was passionate about her house, The Mount, in the Berkshires, Massachusetts, writing to the art historian, dealer and collector Bernard Berenson in 1911 that 'this place of ours is really beautiful; the stillness, the greenness, the exuberance of my flowers, the perfume of my hemlock woods, & above all the moonlight nights of my big terrace, overlooking the lake'.

Described by RWB Lewis, in *Edith Wharton: A Biography*, as the 'first woman of American letters', Wharton wrote in bed each morning from her suite overlooking her Red Garden, which she called her 'Oriental carpet, floating in the sun', as it was laid out in a detailed pattern of lilac and red stocks, and scented dianthus in pink, apricot and cherry.

As well as nine works of non-fiction—on architecture, interior design and gardens—Wharton published twenty-one novels and eleven collections of short stories. However, in 1911, she wrote to the journalist Morton Fullerton: 'Decidedly, I am a better landscape gardener than novelist, and this place, every line of which is my own work, far surpasses *The House of Mirth*.'

A stroke took her life on 11 August 1937; she is buried in the American Cemetery at Versailles.

25 January

Frame the view

In many cultures around the world, the framing of a view is central to garden design. In Chinese gardens, windows decorated with delicately

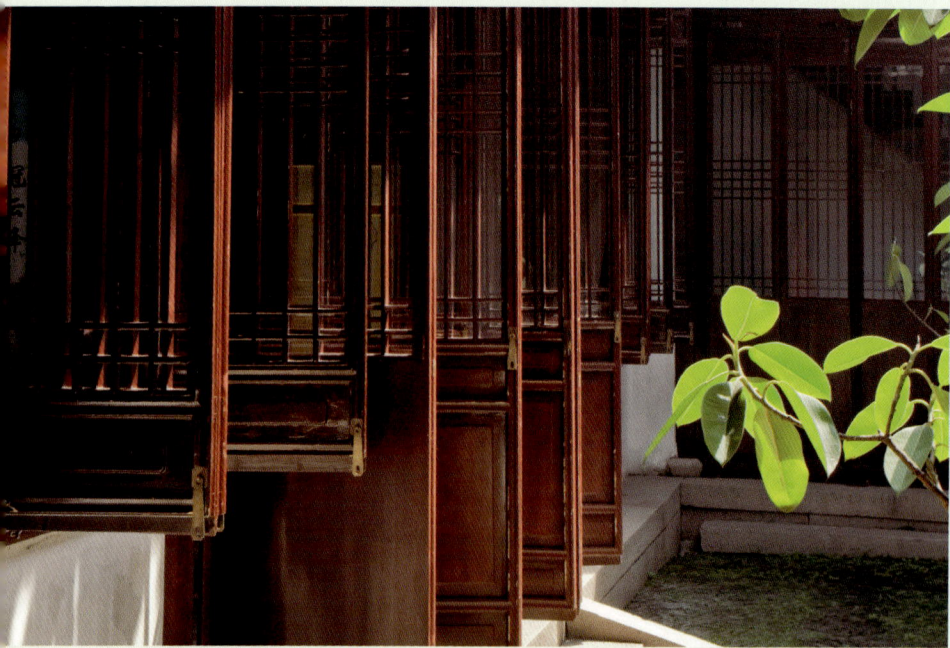

In Suzhou's Garden to Linger In (Liu Yuan), beautiful doors lead into a small courtyard.

carved woodwork, and opening onto a scene, are popular; gaps in walls are enhanced with lacework; and moon gates are used to enclose a view. Intricate paving, and small motifs that decorate railings and roofs, are also used in Chinese garden art.

As well as instruction on the use of water and rockwork, the garden designer, poet and painter Ji Cheng, in *Yuan Ye* (*The Craft of Gardens*), his three-volume treatise on landscape practice and theory, completed in 1634, gives advice on door and window construction, and illustrates hundreds of patterns for latticework.

26 January

Australia Day

Today is Australia Day, to many Australians a celebration of the day on which Captain Arthur Phillip, along with his flotilla of eleven ships holding some 1500 passengers, including 548 male and just 188 female convicts, landed at Bennelong Point, where Sydney's Opera House stands today. Phillip noted, in a letter to Lord Sydney in May 1788, that the land had a 'wild appearance … entirely untouched by cultivation'. It is a very different place two centuries later!

A perfect view of the Opera House and Sydney Harbour bridge from the Royal Botanic Gardens, Sydney

Colour

When I reflect upon my favourite cities of the world, colours and textures come to mind. London is washed in the browns and crimsons of tapestries and textiles; Isfahan, in Iran, is bathed in the soft-pink light of almond blossom; Venice, too, is misted in pink. Melbourne is dressed in the greys and blacks of serious intellectual thought, and Sydney is blue and white, crisp and sparkling.

If months were colours, January would also be, for me, blue and white—the freshest of hues. It is the month that we dream of clear, blue water; the sky is often cloudless, and meals are taken in the garden. China is often blue and white, and set on starched white linen. Hydrangeas are blooming in deepest indigo; delphiniums are filling the flower markets with their cerulean spires; borage is blooming a sky blue; bowls of creamy-white gardenias add their indescribable scent to the house.

Blue—the shades of summer

Wisteria

If you adore wisterias, you may have looked longingly at images of the 140-year-old specimen in Ashikaga Flower Park, north of Tokyo. The wisteria reaches some 500 metres in diameter, and is the largest in the country, and probably in the world. Altogether, the park has more than 160 wisterias, all over 60 years old, which flower in May.

While you and I may not aspire to grow anything as grand as these plants, now is the time to hard-prune wisterias in Australia, particularly if they are still developing the shape and cover you desire: you won't want to

Wisterias will reward summer pruning with a fantastic, scented display in spring.

hard-prune in winter, as you will remove the flower buds that have started to fatten. If your wisteria is well established, providing the required cover, simply pull away any long summer strands that are not contributing to the overall desired shape and frame of this glorious climber.

29 January

Gardens in literature

Gardens and flowers have often been employed to illustrate various themes in literature. Jane Austen used the landscape movement of eighteenth-century England to mock the aspirations of the rising middle class. In *Mansfield Park*, Austen's most 'landscaped' novel, characters who change their gardens for the sake of fashion are derided as '*nouveaux riches*'. The novel's protagonist, Fanny Price, is scandalised by Henry Crawford's 'improvements' to Sotherton, made simply, she feels, for the sake of fashion and to display his new-found wealth.

And George Eliot described bucolic abundance to reflect upon innocence and goodness: she approved of flowers, fruit, herbs and vegetables growing together in glorious profusion. In her novel *Scenes of Clerical Life*, she described 'a charming paradisiacal mingling of all that was pleasant to the eyes and good for food'. The sensibilities of the characters in the novels of Patrick White unfold through their interest in botany and horticulture; in *Voss*, one subject 'is particularly fond of woodland and hedgerow flowers: violets, primroses, anemones … she will venture out in the roughest weather … to see her flowers'.

30 January

Hellebores

Have you divided your hellebores yet? Propagation of plants by division—most often when they are three or four years old—will ensure that each offspring replicates its parent, and is best done towards the end of summer. (Propagation by seed is also possible but will not guarantee an exact reproduction of the parent plant.) To divide hellebores, first remove flower heads as they become spent, to encourage new stem growth; then, using a

Hellebores are no-fuss groundcovers and easy to propagate.

strong fork, lift out the entire plant. Turn it over and divide with a sharp spade or knife. Replant in well-drained soil in the garden, or pot up and keep moist, in a shaded position.

31 January

Lachlan Macquarie

Lachlan Macquarie, born in Scotland on this day in 1762, was the fifth governor of New South Wales, from 1810 to 1821. As well as many glorious buildings created from the abundant sandstone of the Sydney Basin, he gave Australia its first botanic garden, planted around Sydney Harbour, in 1816, to acclimatise and assess new plants from around the world, from other scientific institutions. Three thousand new food plants and fruit trees had been introduced by 1825, including specimens from botanic gardens in India, Mauritius, Great Britain and France.

February

Agapanthus

It's a little sad that a plant with such an evocative name as 'lily of the Nile' could be classed as a weed, but the fact remains that the common agapanthus (*Agapanthus praecox*), native to South Africa, is on Australia's 'don't plant' list. Although it has been the saviour of many a country garden, the agapanthus has been out of favour lately, as it loves our climate so much that it has been known to escape into the bush, taking over from indigenous plants.

The genus *Agapanthus* was established by Charles Louis L'Héritier de Brutelle, a French botanist, in 1788, coincidentally, the same year that New South Wales was first settled by Europeans. On their journey from England to the new colony many settlers collected seeds of the attractive plant for their new homes. If you still have common agapanthus in your garden, the dying flower heads will now be going to seed; if you have not already done so, it's time to cut them off, and dispose of them safely, so that the seeds don't escape into the surrounding environment.

The summer blue of easy-going agapanthus

The range of sterile agapanthus widens with each season, however, so you don't have to forgo this easy-going and colourful summer bloomer. A selection of politically correct agapanthus is available, both by mail order from specialist growers, and in garden nurseries.

2 February

Spring catalogues

Catalogues for spring-flowering bulbs will be starting to drop through your letterbox this month. While it is often difficult, in the heat of summer, to think about what may be flowering in late winter and spring, you will need to order soon if you want to snap up some of the more unusual species and varieties. So, here is the perfect excuse to take some time off from garden work, settle down with a mug of tea, and plan for the cooler seasons. There are many excellent bulb growers—mostly located in the colder parts of the country—that offer a tempting list of treasures available by mail order.

3 February

Grasses

In these times of climate change, and with the threat of drought ever-present, Australian gardeners are always searching for less thirsty species. Grasses, which will be blooming now in masses of waving, feathery plumes, are a solution to this quest. They create height without using excessive lateral space, particularly important in small gardens and courtyards. In borders they provide a look of insouciance; use them in wide rivers of just a few species for a freedom that is bold as well as beautiful. In large gardens they can create a natural, low-maintenance 'prairie' look. And, they thrive on little water.

The choice is vast, from the giant stipas, holding gauzy summer flowers high on tall stems, to the *Miscanthus*, blooming through summer with soft-brown plumes that fade to caramel: the fine-leaved *M.* 'Gracillimus' is one of the decade's must-have plants. The tall-growing reed grass (*Calamagrostis* spp.) is a genus with over 250 species. While several species of fountain grasses are invasive, some cultivars, including *Pennisetum setaceum* 'Rubrum' and 'Atrosanguineum', with burgundy foliage and rose-pink plumes held at

1.5 metres, have undergone rigorous testing, and are said to be sterile. But, in country gardens and suburbs towards the edges of cities, be careful that your borders and meadows of waving, aestivating grasses are not harbouring snakes. And always check out the weeds list (www.weeds.org.au) to make sure you're not planting something that will become a monster!

Mass plant the sterile grasses for a display that changes with the seasons.

4 February

Botanical art

For those among us who cannot draw a straight line, the ancient art of depicting botanical specimens in such perfect detail that they appear alive can hold a deep fascination. In the best examples of botanical art, the plants seem three-dimensional: you can see pollen on anthers, the texture and gloss of the petals. You can almost smell the blooms.

The artist Beverly Allen's exquisite work can be seen at botanic gardens around the country, and in exhibitions and collections worldwide. Scale and perspective are crucial to her work. She strives for botanical accuracy, and fine detail and paint work, making the brush strokes indiscernible. When asked what is needed for the execution of these gorgeous paintings, Beverly nominates patience, and the ability to continue until the work is finished, until all the details are in. Every nuance of texture, every botanical detail is crucial.

Beverly painted the rough tree fern (*Cyathea australis*) for *The Highgrove Florilegium*, published in 2008, a two-volume, limited-edition folio of watercolours illustrating plants grown at Highgrove, in Gloucestershire, the country house of the Prince of Wales. Like all her work, the painting was a life-size image executed from the plant in its natural, growing state.

Beverly conducts four-day workshops each March at the Sydney Royal Botanic Gardens.

5 February

Plumbago

You may not have paid much attention to the humble plumbago (*Plumbago auriculata*), a versatile plant that is so happy in the Australian climate that it has been accused of being 'weedy'. From a genus of fifteen species that are native to South Africa, Central America and South Asia, plumbago thrives during droughts, blooming for months. Over the past few years I've noticed in my neighbourhood a relaxed hedge of the palest of blue plumbagos flowering with the white variety: it is the most charming sight. Also near my house is a crepe myrtle—not pruned, but left to grow into its natural spreading shape—that blooms a deep pink in late February. A deep-blue plumbago (*P. auriculata* 'Royal Cape') is scrambling through it—another stunning combination.

6 February

Figs

Among the most delicious of summer fruits is the fig. It is also a good choice for an espalier, for those gardeners who don't have room for a fully grown tree. *Ficus carica* 'Black Mission', 'Genoa' and 'Brown Turkey' are among the best, as is 'Smyrna', which does not need another variety for pollination. While figs are in season and inexpensive, use them in cooking: preserve them to extend the enjoyment of this luscious fruit.

Fig and almond tart

FOR THE PASTRY
150 g unsalted butter
1 tablespoon caster sugar
1 egg, beaten
250 g plain flour, sifted with pinch salt
1 egg white, beaten

Cream butter and sugar, then add beaten whole egg. Fold this into flour until a soft dough forms. Turn out onto a cold board, knead lightly, wrap in cling wrap and refrigerate for 15 minutes.

Preheat oven to 180°C. Roll out pastry to line a greased 22-centimetre springform tin. Bake blind (place cooking foil on top of the pastry and weigh it down with a layer of beans or rice—this stops the pastry from rising) for 15 minutes. Remove foil and beans; brush pastry with egg white, and return to the oven for a further 5 minutes. Cool before adding filling.

FOR THE FILLING
60 g unsalted butter
5–8 large, ripe figs, stalks removed
4 eggs
100 g caster sugar
100 g almond meal
1 teaspoon vanilla essence
150 ml pouring cream

Preheat oven to 200°C. Melt and cool the butter; set aside. Halve figs and place cut side down on the cooled pastry case. Beat together eggs and sugar; add butter, then almond meal and vanilla essence. Fold in cream. Pour carefully over figs and bake for about 30 minutes, until filling is firm and golden brown. Serve warm with vanilla ice cream.

And this is a wonderful jam that I just have to share with you. It can be spooned between shortbread layers with whipped cream (try it with the macadamia nut shortbread—see 15 November), baked in a cake batter or drizzled on ice cream. Or, serve it with roast lamb!

Fig and ginger conserve

1 kg ripe figs, quartered, and stalks trimmed
1 kg caster sugar
1 large piece ginger (about 3 cm long, or to taste),
    peeled and finely diced
1 teaspoon ground cinnamon
2 star anises (whole)
½ teaspoon ground allspice
zest and juice 2 lemons

Mix all ingredients together and leave to macerate for 1–2 hours in a covered bowl. Simmer for 10 minutes in a heavy-bottomed saucepan, until all sugar is dissolved. Boil rapidly for a further 20–30 minutes, or until jam starts to darken. Remove from heat, take out star anises and discard. Cool jam slightly and then pour into warm sterilised jars. Makes 1 litre.

7 February

Geraniums

It's difficult, I know, but it is time to force yourself to prune your pelargoniums. Sometimes called storksbills, but more commonly known as geraniums, these easy-to-please plants seem to bloom, almost without rest, for much of the year. Taking to them with the secateurs now, however, will reward you with a fabulous show come spring. Remove dead sections and old leaves, and prune to shape, sharing the cuttings with friends and neighbours, for geraniums are extremely easy to propagate. Water in a high-potassium fertiliser. You might consider planting them in a massive jar, or other strong pot, along with star jasmine and wisteria, so that something is always in flower.

Dame Elisabeth

Elisabeth Joy Greene, who later became Dame Elisabeth Murdoch, AC, DBE, was born in Melbourne on this day in 1909. Her tireless work for myriad children's charities, the arts, heritage and horticultural organisations, and education facilities is well known, and she was among a group of horticulturalists, historians and architects instrumental in the formation of the Australian Garden History Society (www.gardenhistorysociety.org.au) in 1980. Often described as Australia's matriarch, Dame Elisabeth has lived

The driveway of lemon-scented gums (*Corymbia citriodora*) at Cruden Farm

and gardened at Cruden Farm, at Langwarrin, south-east of Melbourne, for more than seventy years. Originally laid out, in the early 1930s, by the landscaper Edna Walling, the garden at Cruden Farm now clearly displays Dame Elisabeth's design hand. With its famous sweeping drive of lemon-scented gums, its walled 'garden rooms', wonderful large rose garden—replete also with clematis and perennials—and detailed shrubberies and flower borders, Cruden Farm has been visited by thousands of garden lovers, and, through books and magazines, has been experienced by millions more.

Cruden Farm's rose garden, viewed from across the lake

9 February

Araluen

Public parks and botanic gardens are not simply repositories of plants; they can also bring together groups of people of disparate interests. For example, the Araluen Blues Festival is just one of the events held throughout the year at Araluen Botanic Park (www.araluenbotanicpark.com.au), located in the Darling Range, just east of Perth: the magnificent garden has also become a valued venue for concerts and horticultural shows, including the Chilli Festival in March, and Tulip Time in August.

'Araluen' is an Aboriginal word meaning running, or singing, water. The park is set among tall gums—mainly jarrah and marri—and was the inspiration of a young Perth businessman, John Joseph Simons, who, in the early 1930s, bought the 60 hectares of native forest, with its understorey of grass trees, ferns and orchids, as a place for the city's youth to take part in outdoor activities. Central to the park is an avenue of eighty-nine cypresses, planted to commemorate the number of Young Australia League members who died in World War I. After Simons's death, in 1948, the garden fell into disrepair, until it was rescued in the early 1990s by a group of West Australian garden lovers; it is now owned by the state government and managed by volunteers.

The park contains walking trails, rock pools and reflection pools, and a magnificent curving pergola that is 50 metres long, and has thirty-eight massive cylindrical stone pillars. Mud-spattered notes in Simons's handwriting have been discovered, listing the names of the eighty roses, planted in August 1938, that once graced the pergola, and all but three have been replanted. These include the lovely peach- or apricot-coloured climbing 'Lorraine Lee', bred by the Australian Alister Clark, the blush-pink climbing 'Lady Sylvia' (also known as 'Ophelia') and the climbing 'Souvenir de Mme Boullet'. The once-flowering heritage roses are at their best in early November.

10 February

Camellias

The camellia is surely the most generous—and among the most beautiful—of all flowers. The genus *Camellia* was named to commemorate the contribution to science of Georg Kamel, a Czech-born Jesuit priest who became both a prominent botanist and a missionary to the Philippines in the seventeenth century.

The first of the camellias to bloom, the *C. sasanqua* species, will have started its annual performance already, and will give us months of colour and elegance. 'Setsugekka', with its masses of white fluted flowers on long, supple limbs, is about the first to flower, along with the pink-and-white 'Jennifer Susan' and 'Beatrice Emily'. If you can bring yourself to be ruthless, remove the buds that are forming in clusters of two or three. Leaving just one bud per cluster will result in a larger, healthier bloom.

Many camellias, particularly the sasanquas, with their whippy, flexible stems and branches, are easy to espalier. Use them to cover a bagged wall or an inauspicious boundary. Fade out an unattractive fence by painting it green, then tension galvanised wires across it and plant your camellias about 60 centimetres apart along its base. Once they have finished flowering, in mid-winter, it's time to prune, and then twist the branches along the wires. 'Setsugekka' is particularly successful used in this way.

You can also thread *C. sasanqua* through a hedge of a different genus, or wrap the white-flowering 'Mine-no-yuki' around a simple column to create a striking punctuation point at the end of a walk.

11 February

Butterflies

Among the joys of an insecticide-free garden are the sound of birdsong and the sight of many glorious butterflies drunk on blossom nectar. So many of our native, and exotic, plants attract the birds and the bees—and the butterflies—to the garden. The honeyeaters love grevilleas; callistemons and eucalypts are loved by the brightly coloured lorikeets; the butterflies love buddleias. Birds and butterflies like to rest, and some birds nest, in grasses.

12 February

Charles Darwin

Charles Darwin, the English naturalist, was born on this day in 1809. Although he was educated in medicine at Edinburgh University and then in divinity at Cambridge, Darwin was more interested in natural history, particularly beetles. The publication of *The Voyage of the Beagle*, his account of his five years, from 1831, spent circumnavigating the world on board HMS *Beagle*, made him a household name. On 12 January 1833, at the age of twenty-seven, he sailed into Sydney Harbour. Darwin's observations on the Australian landscape are of interest to any gardener. In January 1836, he travelled from Parramatta to Penrith, and later wrote:

> The extreme uniformity in the character of the Vegetation is the most remarkable feature in the landscape of the greater part of New S. Wales. Everywhere we have an open woodland; the ground being partially covered with a very thin pasture. The trees nearly all belong to one family & have the surface of their leaves placed in a vertical, instead of as in Europe, a nearly horizontal position … Nowhere is there an appearance of verdure, but rather that of arid sterility.

It is not surprising that he was less than enthusiastic about the landscape, as he travelled at the height of summer.

13 February

Herbs

You may not be able to use all the herbs that your garden is producing at the moment, and it's best not to let them go to seed. So, harvest your herbs, use scissors to chop them finely, and freeze them in ice cube trays, in enough water to ensure that they will freeze. Or, you can freeze larger quantities in zip-lock bags. Then you will have fresh herbs to add, easily, to cooking, the year round.

The lovely herb garden at Sissinghurst, in Kent, in the south of England

St Valentine's Day

It's St Valentine's Day, of course: the day when florists' shops sell out of red roses. Among the loveliest and most richly scented are 'Mr Lincoln', a clear red, and 'Peter Frankenfeld'. Both have a stunning fragrance; both, being hybrid tea roses, will flower repeatedly, from early summer and into autumn. Cutting the blooms on long stems will not only make them look lovely in the vase, but will serve as a summer prune, ensuring the next flush of flowers. And 'Mr Lincoln' is one of the varieties of roses somewhat resistant to fungal diseases such as black spot.

The very red rose 'Peter Frankenfeld'

15 February

'Chinese' Wilson

Ernest Henry Wilson, who became well known to garden lovers as the plant hunter Ernest 'Chinese' Wilson, was born on this day in 1876, in the charming Cotswold village of Chipping Camden. In 1897 he started work at the Royal Botanic Gardens, Kew, and at one stage received the Queen's Prize for Botany. From 1899 (the year of his first trip to China) to 1922, he travelled the world searching for plants. The dedication in the first volume of his work *Plant Hunting*, initially published in 1927, perhaps best articulates his interest in the rare and hard-to-find: 'To those of every race and creed who have laboured in distant lands to make our gardens beautiful this volume is dedicated'. Many of the plants we take for granted today were discovered by Wilson, among them maples, rhododendrons, magnolias and camellias.

The handkerchief tree (*Davidia involucrata*), native to China, was brought to England by Ernest Wilson in 1904.

Composition—one of the muses of garden photography

16 February

Garden photography

I'm often asked for advice on taking garden photographs. Thanks to today's easy-to-use digital cameras, producing images of your own garden, or of other people's gardens—to remember good ideas, or important experiences—is possible for everyone. Even with fully automatic cameras, however, there are several elements to keep in mind to maximise the beauty of the photographs you take.

Great pictures evoke an emotional response from the viewer; you could call this the 'gasp factor'. The three keys to good garden photographs are light, composition and colour, in that order. To take great pictures you need to understand these elements, to curtsy to these three muses.

You need look no further than the impressionist painters for clear lessons in light. Monet's *Haystack* series demonstrates how light changes throughout the day and how mood and atmosphere are influenced by that light. Light

can make the most average plant, and even the most ordinary landscape, special. For instance, gathering storm clouds, which at first will prompt you to pack up your camera, may part to allow a magical green light to shine though; capture it, and it will transform a photograph into a work of art. For most photographers, particularly in Australia, where the midday light is so harsh, early morning and late afternoon are the magic hours.

Again, there is no better teacher in composition than the impressionist painter. Notice how a river, or a lane, does not cut through the centre of a painting, but, instead, meanders across it in a diagonal fashion, and how tall poplars frame a view of distant mountains. Keep compositions tight to eliminate distracting details: you are seeking simplicity and balance. 'Edit' is a key word here: you don't want to capture on paper all that you see when you are in the location itself. Also, consider the position of your camera. Move around with the camera: move left, then right. Get down low. Gardens with a strong structure are easier to photograph than more natural spaces: think of box hedges in English gardens. Look for a focal point: use a fountain, a tree or a building to attract the eye.

Colour can be the subject of the photograph, and can transform the ordinary into the extraordinary. The drama of bright, vibrant primary colours can become more important than composition. If the subject is of paler hues, you need texture—dew, perhaps, or the downy surface of a leaf—to ensure a great picture. Keep your eyes open for good colour combinations: pink magnolias flowering above hellebores of a deep red-black, among ribs of hen and chicken fern, with their crimson stems, for example.

Finally, keep your camera handy at all times! While my camera bag, with its large camera body and a variety of lenses, and my tripods, are not always with me, my small automatic camera has a permanent place in my handbag.

17 February

The language of flowers

Flowers speak a language. Victorians and Edwardians, particularly, used flowers to express their feelings. Today we give flowers to convey a message of thanks or love, but are most often unaware that each bloom is part of a

Opposite: Cherry blossom week in Kyoto—colour is the subject

language. Each has significance, apart from its beauty and contribution to the garden: flowers have been used throughout history, and by different cultures, to impart moods and meanings:

Baby's breath symbolises everlasting love.
The bluebell signifies humility.
Borage spells courage.
The eucalyptus is a symbol of protection.
Garlic, perhaps not surprisingly, is a symbol
    of courage and strength.
The gladiolus is a symbol of love at first sight.
Lavender speaks of devotion.
The goblet-shaped blooms of the magnolia
    denote sweetness and beauty.
Narcissus warns of egotism.
Oleander foretells danger.
The rose spells love, of course.
Rosemary is for remembrance.
Sage, the herb, symbolises wisdom.
The tiger lily promises wealth and signals pride.

Take care, then, with your choice of bouquets. Indeed, in some cultures, some flowers symbolise sadness. Calla lilies are traditionally used at funerals, while dark-red roses are, to some, a symbol of mourning.

18 February

Grey-leaved plants

February is often the hottest month of the year, with temperatures reaching 40 degrees or more. There are several plants that are happy in the hot and dry conditions of high summer; they are often grey-leaved, and many are perfect to weave through a border, to bring a colour scheme together or to clip into a hedge.

Our native coastal rosemary (*Westringia fruticosa*) makes a successful hedge in a dry climate, but requires clipping from the get-go if it is to become dense from the base. *Teucrium fruticans* is another grey-leaved plant which,

Greys and blues can tie together different sections of a garden—here, Russian sage (*Perovskia atriplicifolia*).

with regular clipping, makes a great hedge. For an informal look, try hedges of lavender (*Lavandula* spp.), which thrives in a dry climate. You might clip lavender into irregular cloud shapes: that way, should you lose one, the entire hedge will not be ruined. In misty, mountain climates, Russian sage (*Perovskia atriplicifolia*) is more successful. Or, you might use the greys and blues of catmint (*Nepeta × faassenii*) for hedging and to marry the various sections of the garden. The bearded iris (*Iris germanica*), with its soft, glaucous foliage, loves to bake in the sun—although it will have finished flowering by now, of course. The silver-leaved pinks (*Dianthus* spp.) love dry heat. And many succulents are grey-leaved and are happy basking in the sun. The tough and water-wise *Cotyledon orbiculata* and *C. orbiculata* 'Undulatum' bear marvellous silvery leaves and produce tall umbels of apricot-coral bell-shaped flowers in autumn. An added bonus is that the honey-eating birds love them.

19 February

Poultry

Many of us harbour a desire to be self-sufficient. The romantic dream of living off the produce in our back garden—a cornucopia of fruit, herbs and vegetables, all grown effortlessly in our fertile soil (we imagine)—is linked to a deep-seated desire to return to a pure environment and a supposedly simple 'country' way of life. In times of trouble, particularly, we seem to need to create something good from the soil.

Collecting the eggs from our own chooks is part of the dream, and suppliers of chickens, including those who rent out poultry, report a marked increase in recent business. We are all nesting, perhaps.

There are sixty-odd popular pure breeds available, but, if you yearn to keep poultry, you need, firstly, a secure coop, so that the birds will be safe from foxes overnight. The coop, which must be kept clean and dry, needs a covered area for protection from the weather; lay straw over this area, in which your chooks will nest. They need a constant supply of fresh water and organic feed, and should be allowed to range in the garden by day. Feed them kitchen scraps each morning, but clean these up at night so you won't attract vermin.

It is possible to rent chooks before buying, to see if you can cope with the additional daily tasks necessary for caring for them properly. And, if you are really keen, why not join a poultry club?

20 February

Negative ions

As it's February, we are probably all thinking of water—how much of it we have, how much we need, and how we like to swim in it at this time of the year. If we can't fully immerse ourselves in water each day, a water feature, no matter how small, adds a soothing coolness to the garden.

Cultures the world over, and since pre-history, have understood the importance of water in the garden. From the United Kingdom to Iran, Singapore and Australia, water has always featured in landscape design in some way. If you are feeling depressed, slothful and generally disengaged from life, you may need to welcome some negative ions into your day. Ions are particles in the air, and negative ions, found near clear, fresh water, are said to boost the spirits. They are produced through water molecules, so are around moving-water features: cascading waterfalls, clear streams and sparkling, blue oceans. The air around a waterfall contains many more negative ions than air in a car

Feel the benefits of moving water in the garden

or building: that's probably why the sight of a sparkling, crystal-clear ocean makes us want to dive right in.

So, whether you garden in a small city space, or on country hectares, add a water feature. Choose a bowl or a barrel, line a small pool with tiles, or dig an expansive lake, and, if you can create movement, the splashing water will be mesmerising, calming and health-giving.

21 February

Day lilies

In high summer, when it is too hot to do much in the garden, plants that will take care of themselves—that may multiply without becoming weeds, and that require little or no water—become garden stars. Among these hardy troopers is the day lily (*Hemerocallis* spp.), which can be seen massing out in wild meadows and natural plantings in gardens like the Mona Estate, on the Southern Tablelands in New South Wales; in Naumkeag, in the Berkshires,

The double flowering day lily, *Hemerocallis fulva*

west of Boston; and in the natural plantings at Dumbarton Oaks, in Washington, DC. The day lily is so tough you can't kill it: neglect it and it will reward you with continuous blooming in a range of sunset colours, from the yellow of 'Stella d'Oro' to the orange of *H. fulva* and the burgundy of 'Zinfandel'.

22 February

Gardening by the moon

Some people plan their gardening life by the rhythms and cycles of the moon: by its phases and its position in the sky. Since early times, gardening by the moon has been practised by peoples of many cultures who believe that the moon affects not only the oceans but also smaller amounts of water—like the sap in plants and droplets on leaves—which in turn affect the germination and growth of plants. For instance, many gardeners believe you must not plant at the time of a full moon, as growth will occur too quickly; instead, planting when the moon is waning is recommended.

23 February

Fuchsias

Fuchsias. Don't they ever rest? They start blooming in July, continue through August and will perform through spring and summer. All they demand is an east-facing position. They don't like frost, so give them protection if you are determined to hanker after what you shouldn't. Cut them back in late summer, if you can bear to lose the flowers. Among the vast collection of hybrids now available, 'Bianca' is good for training on a wall, while 'Chequerboard' loves being planted in a pot and clipped into a standard. For hanging baskets, choose 'La Campanulata': it blooms white, with a pink corolla.

24 February

A great landscape—Bentley, in northern Tasmania

Dame Sylvia Crowe

Dame Sylvia Crowe established her landscape practice in the United Kingdom after World War II, working on a range of commissions, from sumptuous private estates such as Cottesbrooke Hall in Northamptonshire to environmental projects that included coastal reclamation. In her book *Garden Design*, first published in 1958, she reflected upon unity as a characteristic of good gardening, writing that it is 'a quality found in all great landscapes, based on the rhythm of natural land-form, the domination of one type of vegetation and the fact that human use and building have kept in sympathy with their surroundings'.

25 February

Tea

Water is the most consumed beverage in the world, and tea comes second—not terribly surprising, as tea-drinking forms such an important ritual in many countries around the world. Tea-drinking is thought to have originated in China, in 2737 BC, when Emperor Shen Nung discovered it and extolled its health benefits.

Tea is an evergreen shrub (*Camellia sinensis* var. *assamica* and *C. sinensis* var. *sinensis*, both members of the Theaceae family) and is indigenous to mainland South and South-East Asia, where annual rainfall is high. Tea has been commercially grown in India since 1834, mostly from the large-leaved *assamica* variety, although Darjeeling tea, considered by tea lovers to be the finest of the Indian teas, is of the *sinensis* variety, which was taken to India in the nineteenth century by British planters. Since 1869, when a fungus called coffee rust wiped out the coffee plantations in Sri Lanka (until 1972 known as Ceylon), tea has been that country's main cash crop. (Sri Lankan tea production takes place 'up-country', in evocatively named regions like Kandy, Haputale and Nuwara Eliya.) The soft, new tips and first two or three leaves of the tea bush are used, and are hand-picked each fortnight.

The English habit of afternoon tea, or tea—a light meal at around four o'clock in the afternoon—was initiated by Anna Maria Russell, Duchess of Bedford, in the early nineteenth century, when she began taking a snack in the afternoon to tide her over until dinner.

26 February

More-ish fruit

Here is the recipe for a delicious fruit salad that relies upon cold tea to plump up a variety of dried fruits, including apricots, pears, pineapple and prunes. It's high in calories, which is a shame, as it is very more-ish. It will keep for at least a week.

Dried fruit salad

150 g dried apple
200 g dried peach
220 g dried pear
375 g dessert figs
150 g pitted prunes
170 g dried apricots
4 cups weak black tea
70 g honey (use a single blossom, such as apple) (optional)
dash brandy (optional)
2 tablespoons rosewater (optional)
few leaves lemon verbena
fresh rose petals (optional; ensure they have not been sprayed)

In a glass bowl, layer the fruits and cover with tea, in which you have steeped the lemon verbena, and the rose petals, if used. If required, add a little brandy, the honey and the rosewater. Leave, covered, in the refrigerator for 24–48 hours, and serve with whipped cream, vanilla ice cream and toasted almonds. Serves six to eight.

27 February

'Marie van Houtte'

The climbing tea rose 'Marie van Houtte'

Among the loveliest of all the roses is the climbing tea rose 'Marie van Houtte', named for a member of the horticultural van Houtte family of Ghent, in Belgium. The rose was bred in France, and released in 1871. She is trouble-free, and will now be gearing up for her second flush of rich-cream blooms, which are tinged with pink. To me, she looks good enough to eat, frosted with sugar, for afternoon tea!

28 February

Villas of Lake Como

Do you watch James Bond movies as much for their glamorous locations as for their storylines? The settings seem impossibly fabulous, completely out of reach to most of us. But you don't have to be a movie star to visit one of northern Italy's most breathtaking locations, the Villa del Balbianello, perched atop a terraced promontory on the western shore of Lake Como. It is there that the actor Daniel Craig, in the guise of Bond, convalesced after being assaulted by the evil Le Chiffre in the 2006 version of *Casino Royale*.

Before the movie-makers arrived, Lake Como (perhaps the best known of all the Italian lakes, and set among dramatic, snow-capped mountains that crash into its blue waters) was patronised by princes and cardinals. In the sixteenth century, villas were built on its shores by industrial and banking families drawn to the unique setting for their holiday retreats. Charles Dickens, Edith Wharton, George Sitwell and Henry James were among the throng of American and British literati who descended on the lake in the late nineteenth and early twentieth centuries. Lake Como was, wrote James, 'fairly wallowing in libretto'. Bellini composed his *Norma* and *La Sonnambula* on its shores, Rossini his *Tancredi*, and Verdi part of his *La Traviata*.

Once the site of a thirteenth-century Franciscan monastery, Villa del Balbianello was created for the ambitious Cardinal Angelo Durini in the late eighteenth century, before eventually being renovated for the explorer Guido Monzino in the 1970s. The estate was bequeathed to the State in 1988, and is now cared for by the Fondo per l'Ambiente Italiano, an organisation somewhat akin to Australia's National Trust.

'The Italian garden must be studied in relation to the house, and both in relation to the landscape', wrote Edith Wharton, in her *Italian Villas and*

Their Gardens, first published in 1904; 'they are part of the same composition'. At Villa del Balbianello the relationship between the surrounding mountains, the garden and the lake it overlooks is all-important; it seems as if they were created together.

A winding path, shaded by an allée of precisely pruned plane trees, their trunks clothed in clipped ivy, leads the visitor up the steep slope from the charming landing jetty at the base of the garden to the first terrace, with its wisteria-draped railings. On the main lawn, in spring, the bare, twisted branches of the planes form a tracery against the clear blue sky; their crowns provide lush canopies for shade in high summer. The expansive terrace is protected by a stone balustrade decorated with urns of cascading geraniums, their red blooms in perfect counterpoint to the burned umber wash on the villa walls behind, and to the intense blue of the water below. In front of the villa, holm oaks are carefully pruned to ensure the view is not compromised, while a backdrop of obelisk-like cypresses introduces the woodland that clothes the steep mountains in the background.

Villa del Balbianello, on the western shore of Lake Como

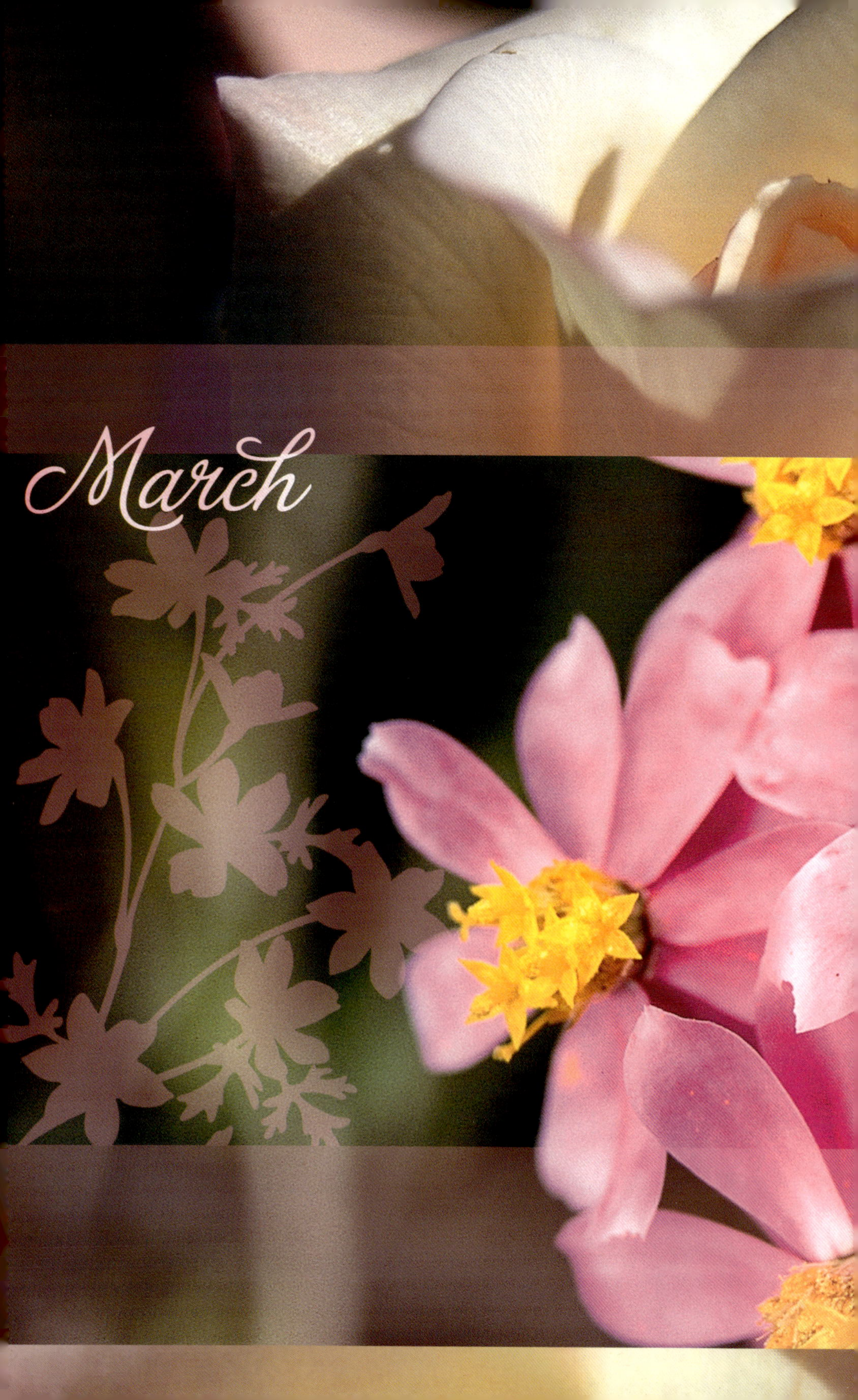
March

Dahlias

While dahlias can be grown from seedlings, cuttings or tubers, only the tubers can be relied upon to grow true to the parent. Dahlias are heavy feeders: prepare the soil a fortnight before propagating by adding aged manure.

The tubers can be lifted after the plants have died down in autumn, or after the first frost blackens the foliage. When dividing tubers, make sure you have at least one 'eye' present to ensure new growth. They should be stored, in sawdust, out of the sun and away from damp and rodents. Re-plant the tubers in late spring, in rich soil, at a depth of about 8 centimetres, in a sunny, sheltered position. Apply fertiliser when the plants reach about 30 centimetres, and, for award-winning results, use a high-potassium liquid fertiliser every two weeks after the buds form.

Autumn finds dahlias blooming

Fabulous colour

While it is still summer in much of the country, in some cooler areas, the dahlia, 'king of the autumn', is at its flamboyant best. It has been out of favour for the past few decades, but new varieties have won the dahlia a place in even the smartest gardens. There are not many plants as generous as the dahlia, which keeps on flowering, and flowering, through late summer and almost into winter, in an extraordinary range of colours, shapes and sizes. Be warned, though: snails and slugs also love them!

Dahlias can be introduced into gentle colour schemes, or the richer reds and oranges team well with the tropical tones of cannas and gingers. Hot-pink dahlias look wonderful with the pinks of cleomes and roses, and with the lime green of *Canna* 'Striata'. Many dahlias start flowering in mid summer, among them 'Fire Mountain', with its pure-red double flowers and black foliage, and 'Bishop of Llandaff', with its red semi-single flowers and stunning dark foliage. The latter was developed in the 1920s and named after the Reverend Joshua Pritchard Hughes, Bishop of Llandaff, but it did not regain favour until the 1980s. Other dahlias popular today include 'Yellow Hammer', the apricot 'Heat Wave', and 'Tally Ho', with its orange blooms and green- to pewter-coloured foliage.

Cannas can team with other hot colours to create exuberant garden schemes.

3 March

A clear sense of place—near Beechworth, in northern Victoria

4 March

Apples in season

There is surely nothing as delicious as a freshly harvested apple. Sweet and crisp, new-season apples are packed with pure goodness. 'Gala' apples are appearing now in markets and fruit shops. The skin of this variety ranges from pale golden yellow with a red blush to solid pink. The juicy 'Golden Delicious', with greenish-yellow to lemon-yellow skin and creamy-white flesh, is available from now until December. It is excellent for baking as it doesn't fall apart. The 'Jonathan' is also in season, and will be available until May.

Later maturing varieties include 'Pink Lady' apples, which are at their best in May, crisp and dripping with juice, their pure-white flesh sweet. The 'Braeburn'—a good choice for baking and storing—is also most delicious in May. The deep-pink 'Sundowner' is late-maturing, along with the green 'Mutsu', with its crisp flesh with the scent of passionfruit—my favourite apple. 'Fuji', bred in Japan, with high sugar levels and pink-blushed cerise skin, is available from April to September.

Eat them in season—'Pink Lady' apples

5 March

Design by hose

Use a garden hose to create a template when thinking about new garden beds. You can lay out the hose where you think the edge of bed should be, and leave it in place for a few days while you consider, and perhaps adjust, its shape. I like to fill in the void created within that outline with newspaper and mulch so that I can image the scale and bulk of the final garden bed.

6 March

Chillies

Chilli seeds were first transported to Europe from South America by Christopher Columbus. Since then, chillies been cultivated throughout the world, adding essential 'zing' to a range of cuisines. Among the easiest of vegetables to grow, chillies, which come in a range of colours and shapes, have a place in every vegie garden. Along with other members of the colourful *Capsicum* genus, including the cayenne, Tabasco and bell peppers, chillies are rich in vitamin C. In many climates, chillies are treated as an annual, but in temperate climates, if they are trimmed back at the end of winter and dressed with compost and mulch, they may produce a second crop.

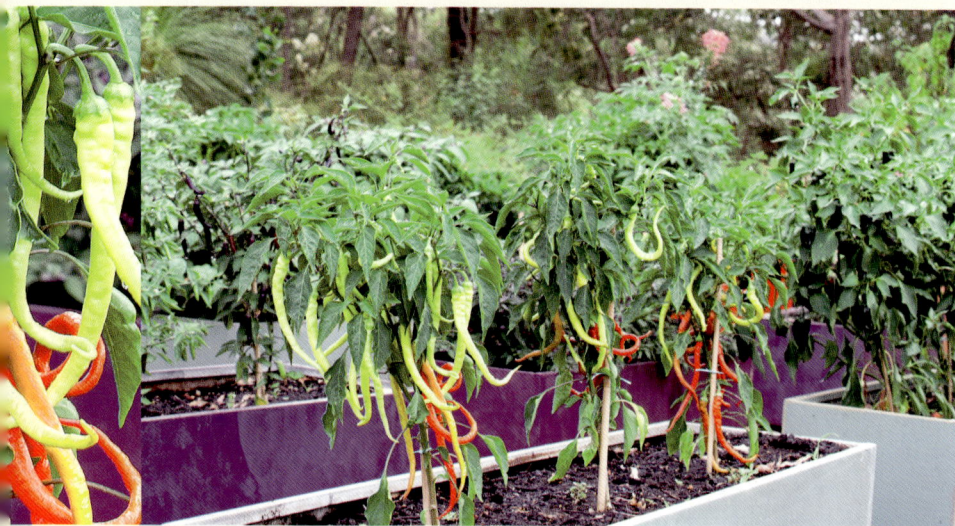

The Chilli Garden at Araluen Botanic Garden

7 March

Harper's Mansion

You'll have to visit in spring if you want to see the lilac, crab-apples and other fruit trees in full bloom around Harper's Mansion (www.harpersmansion .com), in the New South Wales Southern Highlands town of Berrima. But it is in March that the Old Fashioned Fair is held in the grounds, when the climbing roses are in the midst of their 'autumn flush', and the catmint that edges the winding gravel paths is still a mass of purple blossom, and buzzing with bees.

James Harper, an innkeeper and district constable, built this elegant Georgian house, set on 45 hectares, in 1834; it was the most significant building in the town, prompting his neighbours to dub it 'Harper's Mansion'. Once he had cleared the land of its native vegetation, Harper created an extensive garden, with flower beds dressing the front of the house, and a kitchen garden and orchards laid out at the rear. After Harper's death, in 1845, the house had a succession of tenants, and fell into some disrepair. Eventually sold to the National Trust of Australia in 1978, it was restored under the direction of heritage architect Clive Lucas, who noted, in 1984, the remains of 'a squared cottage garden in front of the house with an axial path and evidence of a fence and gateposts'. The garden was restored using this template and reflecting the writings of the Scottish botanist and landscaper John Claudius Loudon, the most influential and fashionable garden writer of the nineteenth century.

Harper's Mansion at Berrima, New South Wales

8 March

The windflower

No matter when Easter arrives, Japanese windflowers (*Anemone japonica*) seem to be blooming in clouds of white or pink. It is not surprising, then, that they are sometimes called Pasque flowers, although this is also the common name for *A. pulsatilla*. Windflowers can grow to some 3 metres

Japanese windflowers always seem to bloom close to Easter.

in height, and, belying their elegant, somewhat fragile-looking disposition, seem to cope with drought and will tolerate early frosts. They look beautiful teamed with Russian sage, and allowed to collapse with insouciance over loose hedges of lavender, or more severely clipped box.

9 March

Vita

Victoria May Sackville-West was born on this day in 1892. A prolific writer and great gardener, she wrote many gardening books and, from 1947, influenced thousands of English gardeners through her column in London's *Observer*. She married the writer, diplomat and amateur architect Harold Nicolson in 1913, and together they created much-admired and often-copied gardens at Sissinghurst Castle, in Kent, which remain among the world's most visited gardens. Set around an Elizabethan tower and series of separate buildings, the gardens are a mix of impressive structure and layout—often said to be the work of Harold—and exuberant, virtuoso planting schemes, which are attributed to Vita (as Sackville-West was known). Roses, clematis and plantings of perennials in myriad colour schemes, along with herb gardens, the 'nuttery', wild meadows, orchards, woodlands and plantings of special trees, all contribute to the Sissinghurst magic. The famous White Garden, with its central arbour of white roses and its plantings in white, silver and green, has been copied by gardeners around the world.

Sissinghurst Castle

10 March

Possums

Mem Fox's bestselling children's book *Possum Magic* was first published on this day in 1983. With exquisite illustrations by Julie Vivas, the book has been continuously in print ever since. Grandma Poss and little Hush are cute and lovable, but if you have real possums in your garden, you may not feel so kindly towards them. There are several ways to deter these destructive creatures from helping themselves to your autumn roses, chewing your fruit and stripping your precious trees of leaves as they run along the possum highway: your front fence! Hanging old CDs from trees is one method: they seem not to like the reflection of the moving discs, at least until they become accustomed to them. Girdles of plastic around tree trunks prevent them from climbing, and keeping branches clear of the roof stop them from leaping onto it in the middle of the night. Also, they seem to dislike the smell of Dynamic Lifter.

11 March

Californian tree poppy

The Californian tree poppy (*Romneya coulteri*) loves hot, dry climates, and flowers with large white papery blooms. It will be getting straggly about now, so cut back hard when most of the flowering is over. Give it a light feed and a deep water. It is not a long-lived plant, so enjoy it while it thrives and plant another when it turns up its toes.

12 March

André Le Nôtre

Perhaps the most important landscaper of the seventeenth century, André Le Nôtre, was born on this day in 1613. From a family of French gardeners, from 1645 to 1700 he was landscape architect to Louis XIV of France. While his first recorded design was for the Orangerie at Fontainebleau, in 1645, he is most famous for the construction of the park at the Palace of Versailles. He was also responsible for the vistas of France's most famous boulevard, the Champs Élysées, and for many public parks and gardens, including St James's Park in London.

13 March

The Eucharist lily

You won't be surprised to learn that the Eucharist lily, also known as the Amazon lily (*Eucharis amazonica*), is native to South America. It is a beautiful, elegant creature, and it will be flowering now. Each bulb produces one white, scented flower held on a spire 30 centimetres high. Its natural habitat is the rainforest floor, where it is moist and shady; the lily is frost-tender. Plant new bulbs in winter, flush with the soil level, and feed them in spring. You can propagate by breaking off baby bulbs from mature plants in summer, but remember, like many autumn-flowering bulbs, the Eucharist lily likes to be crowded.

Jonathan Myles-Lea

When the artist Jonathan Myles-Lea creates a painting of a house and garden, he is 'writing a biography' for its owners. His exquisite works are executed in such detail that he knows, on walking around the garden a few years later, if even a pot plant has been moved. He has completed more than fifty commissions around the world.

Jonathan Myles-Lea's exquisite depiction of the Manor House at Upton Grey (photograph courtesy Prudence Cuming Associates Ltd)

His eye for intricate detail is demonstrated in his painting of the Manor House at Upton Grey, in England, whose owners John and Rosamund Wallinger have meticulously restored the garden, which was originally designed by the Art and Crafts movement's Gertrude Jekyll. Myles-Lea has included personal details: insets show items that are too small to be seen in detail in the main picture. There is the gravestone for Charles Holme, Jekyll's head gardener, who worked on site, for instance; John Wallinger sits reading *The Financial Times*; the boules court is also depicted, as is Rosamund's poultry and her much-loved 'Lady Waterlow' rose.

A Myles-Lea commission begins with a visit to the garden; a detailed survey is followed by preliminary drawings, and then a sepia wash on canvas. Layer upon thin layer of colour is then applied, before the detail is drawn in with fine sable brushes, sometimes of just a single hair. The frame, which aims to reflect the period of the house, is gilded, ebonised, and then covered in a wax polish. Everything in a Myles-Lea painting is correct, from the rhubarb forcers in a kitchen garden to the trees in the orchard. The result is exquisite work that will still be beautiful in several hundred years.

15 March

Apples

Try this apple cake, delicious served warm, with ice cream and cream.

Apple sauce cake

200 g unsalted butter

500 g brown sugar

4 eggs

1 teaspoon vanilla essence

2 cups self-raising flour, sifted with 1 pinch each nutmeg and cinnamon

2 cups apple sauce

Grease a 22-centimetre springform tin. Preheat oven to 180°C. Cream butter and sugar, beat in eggs, and add vanilla essence. Fold in flour and spices. Spoon half the batter into tin and level. Cover with apple sauce. Top with remaining batter and bake 1 hour, or until a skewer, inserted in the centre, comes out clean.

16 March

Autumn chores

Autumn means a lot of work in the garden, tidying, weeding, mulching and preparing it for a winter rest, so that you will reap the benefits of a healthy and well-ordered garden come spring. You will be planting bulbs, picking fruit to freeze or bake, dividing perennials, giving a last mow to the lawn and cleaning garden tools, ready for any repairs that can be carried out during winter. And it's time to harvest the very last of your tomatoes, which, while they may be clinging to the vine, along with the last of your summer chillies, may not ripen now.

17 March

St Patrick's Day

Do you remember finding a four-leaf clover as a child? A mutation found on white clover, a four-leaf clover occurs on one in 10 000 stalks. It is a symbol of good luck, particularly for those with Irish heritage. The three-leaf shamrock is the symbol of St Patrick, whose feast day is today.

Sweet peas clamber up supports in Barbara Labb's garden in November.

Many gardeners believe that St Patrick's Day is the day by which you should have planted your sweet peas. In warmer climates and coastal areas, however, warm soils will rot the seeds, and Anzac Day (25 April) is the final date by which they must go in. In cool areas, sweet pea seeds can also be planted in spring. Sow into moist soil, water, and then wait until the seedlings emerge before you water again. Support seedlings on teepees or trellises of twigs.

18 March

The Isle of Capri

The next time I venture to Capri, the island in the Bay of Naples, it will be in very early spring, or late autumn. It is a gorgeous island, dripping with bougainvillea and adored by nineteenth- and twentieth-century writers and artists, but now a little loved to death by tourists, particularly between May and October.

The most famous garden on Capri belongs to the Villa San Michele, an extraordinary feat of engineering, constructed as it is across several terraces, on the ruins of a villa once owned by Tiberius, the Roman emperor. Built at the end of the nineteenth century for the Swedish physician Axel Munthe, San Michele enjoys walkways of evergreens laid out on several levels and pots of succulents and brightly flowering pelargoniums. The views from the gardens and terraces are fabulous.

19 March

Bonsai

If you long for a wide landscape on which to gaze from your kitchen window, but don't have hectares in which to garden, bonsai, the art of training plants—by pruning and wiring—into miniature shapes and sizes, may well be the answer. Originally restricted to creating dwarf trees and practised only by the elite, today bonsai includes *penjing*, the art of creating a world in miniature, and, since the early twentieth century, has had followers around the globe. Bonsai is a Japanese word that translates as 'planted in a container'. It is known as *bunjai* in Korea and *punsai* in China, where the art began in around 1000 BC. During the Kamakura Period (1192–1333), bonsai was taken to Japan, where the technique was developed.

Among the easiest plants to train are maples, conifers—including the Japanese black pine and Chinese juniper—and beech; azaleas and camellias are also popular. A variety of special pruning scissors is used for trimming branches and roots into the shapes required. As well as a single, beautiful specimen in a receptacle, bonsai can also incorporate a woodland of tiny trees, small mountains and moss-covered rocks, all arranged in a wide, shallow dish. You can imagine that you are looking at forests and mountain paths: a perfect world in a pot.

20 March

The Japanese maples are among the richest of the autumn colouring trees.

Autumn

Today is, technically, the first day of autumn, when the March equinox occurs, at the moment when the centre of the sun is vertically above the equator. And a country gardener told me that she was always taught to feed her camellias when the football season starts and, again, when it ends. Well, the footie season has just started.

21 March

Bamboo

As you might imagine from its name, *Dendrocalamus giganteus* is the world's largest bamboo. Native to Myanmar, this giant among grasses can reach 60 metres in height. A massive example of it grows in the Royal Botanical Gardens of Peradeniya, in Sri Lanka.

At the other end of the scale, the tough evergreen sasa grass, or dwarf bamboo (*Shibataea kumasaca*), must be among the world's smallest bamboo. Used extensively in Japanese gardens, providing an easy-care but lush ground cover in place of a high-maintenance lawn, this bamboo is in a genus of eight species that can survive temperatures as low as minus 10 degrees Celsius. It can be found in woodland gardens, covering slopes, spreading out between rocks at the edges of gravel gardens, and as a living mulch in pot plants.

Sasa grass is among the smallest of the bamboos and good as a groundcover.

22 March

Community gardens

Although community gardens don't have a long history in Australia (the first were established in Victoria in the 1970s), they are becoming increasingly popular as more people decide to eat food that has not been treated with pesticides and herbicides. With backyards becoming smaller—and, often, smarter—as large house blocks fall victim to population expansion and the developer's dollar, and as family dynamics change to include two working parents, vegetable gardens are not always part of the suburban garden. The answer is the community garden, often a home away from home for plot custodians, incorporating small sheds replete with the tools of tea-making, and with chairs and umbrellas ready for rest when the garden work is done.

Communication with friends and neighbours and a sense of belonging are central to community gardening, and councils are increasingly recognising their importance. The Australian City Farms and Community Gardens Network (www.communitygarden.org.au) started in 1996, and provides information for community gardeners around the country.

23 March

Entrances and fences

Garden designer Kath Carr once told me that she considers the entrance to be the most important element in any garden, reasoning that if it is unsightly, passers-by will form a poor opinion of the garden-maker inside. While this may seem a little severe, Carr has a point: like it or not, your front garden sets the tone for your property. A pleasing entrance—in the city your fence, gate and front garden—speaks volumes about the dynamics and demographics beyond. The fence is not an innocent bystander in the meanings carried by a garden. It conveys information on the taste, culture and circumstances of the owner.

Drive around suburbs in any Australian town or city and you can date a property even before you open the gate: front fence styles have changed over the decades in keeping with architectural fashions. The earliest paintings and photographs of gardens in Australia show a wooden picket fence as the favoured means of enclosing the front garden. Around the turn of the nineteenth century, with the building of Federation or Queen Anne Revival houses, complementary, decorative fretwork became popular. Woven-wire fences appeared, allowing passers-by glimpses of the front garden; today they can also be made from Colourbond, or even galvanised iron mesh. High walls to ensure greater privacy became common in the late twentieth century, as the smaller footprint of house and land blocks meant that outdoor courtyards became extensions of indoor living spaces.

Beautiful entrances are an important introduction to your garden. Here, left at Holker Hall, England, and right, Bebeah, Mount Wilson, New South Wales.

24 March

Potatoes

The average Australian consumes about 65 kilograms of potatoes and potato products each year, so it makes economic sense to grow your own! In warm climates, potatoes are sown in autumn and winter for a spring harvest, after which a second crop is planted. In cold, frost-prone areas, they are planted between early spring and summer, so now is the time to lift your potatoes in those areas. Unless you are feeding large numbers, don't pull out the whole plant; rather, dig out the tubers once the leaves start to die right off. 'Bandi-cooting' is an old-fashioned term that means putting your hand under the soil to break off just one potato.

You can grow potatoes in deep polystyrene boxes on a balcony in a sunny spot, or, in a small garden, within a circle of chicken wire for a no-dig potato tube. Add a combination of compost, old manure, some slow-release ferti-liser and good potting mix. Plant seed potatoes, bought from your nursery, at a depth of about 10 centimetres. As the leaves emerge, add more compost and straw around the plant to ensure that it develops tubers up the stem. Fertilise with a potassium-rich product; nitrogen-rich fertilisers will produce leaves at the expense of tubers. The leaves will flower and die back, telling you that the spuds are ready to harvest. Take new potatoes a month after the flowers die, and old potatoes when the leaves have died.

Among the many varieties available for different cooking methods are the waxy 'Kipfler', 'Bintje', 'Nicola' and 'Dutch Cream', which are all good for boiling and steaming; 'King Edward' is a floury variety that is used for mash and roasting. Potatoes are full of nutrients, and, if you resist too much butter, contain few kilojoules.

25 March

The Yangtze River

The mountains of the Three Gorges section of the Yangtze River, in China, are among the most breathtaking examples of the country's picturesque landscape. Such impressive surroundings have created in the Chinese people a reverence for, and understanding of, nature, and have moved artists and scholars throughout the centuries to articulate China's beauty in artworks and words. This reverence is also demonstrated in many of China's great gardens, which often include ornate rockwork, designed to reflect the soaring, mist-shrouded peaks of the mountain areas. Rocks, symbolic of human spirituality, are also associated with immortality.

On the Yangtze River

Produce markets

I adore flower and produce markets. Wherever I am in the world, whether in my home town of Sydney, or in one of my favourite cities in France, Italy, England or Iran, I head, first, to the market. It is there that you see the fabric of a place, its people, its culture, its commerce: its heart. In Australia the burgeoning Farmers' Market movement honours fresh produce and underlines the value we place upon the love and labour that our growers bring to the food they provide. In Sydney, I often visit the Fox Studios farmers' market, near Centennial Park, on a Wednesday morning, to buy armfuls of the freshest (and cheapest) flowers you will find in the city. Or, I head out at dawn to the wholesale flower market at Flemington: this is a fascinating experience with growers from around the state selling their produce. Each Australian city has its equivalent market.

In Paris, in the Marché de Buci, on the Left Bank, I will sit at a sidewalk cafe for hours, nursing a large cup of coffee and watching housewives quibbling over the fruit, tasting the cheeses and selecting cuts of meat. In the south-west of France, my favourite market is in the medieval town of Figeac. In Florence, I visit the marvellous covered market from which you can eat like a gourmet. And in Alexandra, just south of the Potomac River in Washington, DC, the Saturday farmers' market is a joy.

The French town of Figeac hosts a wonderful produce market.

27 March

Neighbours

These days, many of us no longer know our neighbours. Once, cups of sugar, produce, garden cuttings—and gossip—were exchanged over the garden gate or fence. A garden 'look', or vernacular, was created in a suburb as neighbours swapped cuttings. These days, with many more women working, land prices rising and gardens becoming smaller, suburbs do not enjoy the same sense of community. In a move to encourage us to engage more with those in our neighbourhood, the last Sunday in March has become National Get to Know Your Neighbour Day (www.neighbourday.org). The slogan is 'The community you want starts at your front door', and organisers encourage people to introduce themselves to other residents in their street, particularly to older people and to anyone who lives alone. They also suggest swapping telephone numbers for use in an emergency and agreeing to keep in contact. And, why not swap eggs, vegies, flowers and cuttings?

28 March

Green tomatoes

If you have plenty of unripened tomatoes, along with a few chillies hanging on, in your garden, it's time to make green tomato and chilli jam.

Green tomato and chilli jam

3–4 brown onions, finely diced
garlic (to taste), crushed
2 tablespoons olive oil
chillies (to taste, and depending on the variety;
   the seeds provide most of the heat), chopped
few tablespoons brown sugar (to taste)
1–2 kg green tomatoes, chopped
mixed spices, including ground cloves, nutmeg, cinnamon

Fry onions and garlic in oil. Add spices and chillies and fry for a few minutes, then stir in sugar and cook for a few minutes more. Add tomatoes and simmer for 20 minutes. Once the jam has reduced to the consistency you prefer, cool and bottle in sterilised jars. I also freeze several quantities in sturdy plastic containers. Serve with a variety of cold meats (it is particularly good, I think, with ham).

29 March

Edwin Lutyens

Edwin Landseer Lutyens was born in London on this day in 1869. He became one of Britain's greatest architects, famous for his country houses, with their exuberant gardens, which he designed in collaboration with Gertrude Jekyll. Lutyens created a landscape structure of stone balustrades, rills and staircases, while, at the same time, Jekyll softened the designs with plantings. From 1912 Lutyens was instrumental in the design of the city of New Delhi, in India.

Hestercombe in Somerset, England, among the most successful of the Lutyens–Jekyll collaborations

30 March

Sweet potato

Did you know that you can eat the leaves of many of the root vegetables? Kumera, or sweet potato, which we love for its bright-orange, sweet tuberous roots, bears heart-shaped leaves which are edible: sweat them in a few table-spoons of hot water, or toss them for a few minutes in butter. Add flaked sea salt and a knob of cold butter. You can treat the leaves of beetroot and even of grapevines in the same way.

31 March

Tachibana-no-Toshitsuna

We learn about great furniture, beautiful china and fine textiles by observing the best examples of their kind; about good writing by reading the classics, and about wonderful art by looking at the works of the world's finest artists. One of the best ways to learn about good garden design is by visiting great gardens—a tradition that goes back centuries. In *Sakuteiki* (*Notes on Garden Making*), one of the world's earliest manuals of garden design, Tachibana no Toshitsuna, its eleventh-century author, advises: 'Recall the vistas of various famous places, select what attracts you and add your own interpretation. It is best to use this as a theme to design the whole of the garden while adding just the right amount of changes'.

This lovely sculpture at Windyridge garden, Mount Wilson, New South Wales, catches your eye.

April

1 April

Melbourne International Flower and Garden Show

While an Indian summer often lingers during early April—although in mountain areas cooler winds are rustling leaves as they develop a kaleidoscope of feisty autumn colours—Australia's most ambitious garden event, the Melbourne International Flower and Garden Show (www.melbflowershow .com.au), gets under way within the World Heritage–listed Royal Exhibition Building and the surrounding South Carlton Gardens. It features the latest in landscape design and horticulture: there are 'show gardens', book launches, question and answer panels, new plant releases and an extensive array of garden retail products.

2 April

Pears

Pears will be hanging on the trees now, and are inexpensive in the fruit markets. Bake them, bottle them, or slice and freeze them. Or, use them in this delicious cake:

'Beurre Bosc' pears, left, and 'Williams', right

Pear upside down cake

FOR THE TOPPING
5 pears, peeled and quartered
7 pecan nuts, halved
60 g butter
100 g brown sugar

FOR THE CAKE
60 g butter, melted
125 g plain flour
½ teaspoon bicarbonate of soda
pinch salt
125 g brown sugar
90 g black treacle
1 egg
½ cup milk
2 teaspoons cinnamon
1 teaspoon ginger
¼ teaspoon nutmeg
pinch ground cloves

Preheat oven to 180°C. Line a 24-centimetre springform tin with cooking foil, then with greaseproof paper, to prevent the topping from leaking. Arrange pear quarters on base of tin, round side down. Put pecan nut halves between pears. Melt together butter and brown sugar, and pour evenly over pears and pecans.

Mix all cake ingredients in an electric mixer until well combined. Pour over pears and topping. Bake for 1 hour, or until a skewer inserted into the centre of the cake comes out clean. Allow cake to cool slightly in tin, then turn out and serve warm with clotted cream.

3 April

Graham Stuart Thomas

The much-admired rosarian, writer and garden designer Graham Stuart Thomas was born on this day in 1909. Among the many gardens that he designed is the national collection of heritage roses at Mottisfont Abbey, a twelfth-century Augustinian priory in the south of England. Established in 1972, the collection comprises some 300 varieties of roses, planted on the site of a kitchen garden that had supplied Mottisfont with fruit, vegetables and cut flowers for more than two centuries. Designed as a series of squares and rectangles edged with box, lavender, catmint and dianthus, the rose garden is a jewel box of colour, form, texture and scent. Wonderful perennial borders create wide ribbons around the perimeter and are backed with mellow pink-brick walls covered in roses. Rustic structures—arches, ladders, tripods and pergolas—support more roses, all accompanied by a variety of clematis.

While the garden is most famous as the site of heritage roses, its collection has been expanded recently to include many early twentieth-century, repeat-flowering tea and hybrid tea roses. The phenomenally successful varieties by the English breeder David Austin—which have the voluptuous form and scent of the old roses, but are more resistant to disease, have a broader colour spectrum and are repeat-flowering—have also been added. Among the apricots, pinks and yellows is the glorious golden rose bred for, and dedicated to, Graham Stuart Thomas, who died on 16 April 2003.

The walled rose garden at Mottisfont

4 April

Autumn excitement

With changes in colour and texture—in leaves, flowers and seeds—grasses take on added importance through autumn and winter, the quieter seasons. After they have flowered, leave their seed heads in place, to turn gold, russet and red: they look stunning silhouetted against a glowering winter sky. Or, cut them back ruthlessly if a neat and tidy garden is what you most desire.

5 April

The tussie mussie

Say it with flowers. If roses speak of love, lavender warns of jealousy and lilies signify purity, the tussie mussie surely says it all. This posy of herbs and flowers is a complete conversation: a romantic poem, a love letter or simply a gesture of friendship. Popular with brides since Elizabethan times, and carried by judges in the Victorian era to ward off disease (and the evil intentions of criminals), a tussie mussie remains easy to make. Simply select a central 'hero' flower (such as a rose) and arrange around it a variety of flowers (such as lavenders and violets) and herbs (the natural-remedy medicine chest). Hold it all in place with an elastic band or florist's tape, then wrap it in tissue or a piece of lace, hide your workings with a ribbon, and wait for the appreciation!

6 April

Cherry blossom

Japan's Cherry Blossom Week occurs early this month, when the *sakura*, or cherry trees, are blooming. Throughout the country, canals, rivers and roads are lined with these elegant trees, which bend black, outstretched limbs towards the ground and often flower early, on bare branches; clouds of pale single blossoms soften austere wooden temples, and hillsides are lit by the blooms. The Japanese, masters of clarity and simplicity, understatement and refinement, also revere the flamboyant excesses of nature which herald the changing of the seasons. *Sakura*, the unofficial national flower of Japan, is an enduring symbol of spring, central to notions of grace, elegance, delicacy and fleeting beauty.

The ethereal blossom of the cherry tree in Kyoto, during *hanami*, or blossom viewing

7 April

Ravello

The roses are blooming in Italy's south, where is it spring, of course. One of the country's most beautiful areas is the Amalfi Coast, a few hours' drive south of Rome. There, the ancient town of Ravello, founded in the sixth century, perches, somewhat precariously, atop Dragon Hill. The town is an atmospheric mix of alleyways, roofed passages lined with shops and lime-washed facades that fold out from a central square.

One of Ravello's most famous sites is the Villa Cimbrone, purchased, in 1904, by Ernest William Beckett, an art dealer who later became Lord Grimthorpe. Local architect Nicola Mansi was then employed to create an expansive park, central to which is the Walk of Eternity. Vistors begin their exploration of the gardens at a simple entrance gate, moving through a vine-covered arch and on, by a curving, narrow path edged with large urns bursting with cordylines, until it opens into a wide, generous avenue. From there it is possible to look down upon expansive lawns, collections of important

The view from Villa Cimbrone, Ravello, in Italy

statuary and rose gardens: it all creates a calm, restrained atmosphere. The walk, bordered by flowering oleander and shaded by ancient stone pines, eventually arrives at the Terrace of Infinity, a belvedere looking out to the sea: the views are simply astonishing.

8 April

Fruit-tree pruning

It's time to prune fruit trees such as apricots that produce on one-year-old wood, to encourage fruit production and for shape and ease of management. Take care not to remove the short spurs that will produce flowers. Fertilise the trees after pruning.

It's also time to spray fruit trees for sap-sucking pests such as aphids and thrips. Spray fortnightly throughout autumn with a horticultural oil or Natrasoap. In cold climates where the slimy, black pear and cherry slug can be a problem, remember to spray apple, pear and quince trees with a commercial copper solution at leaf fall. Spray them again in early spring, at budburst. Also, apply a light feed to your citrus, and keep up the water as the fruits fatten, to ensure that they are thin-skinned and juicy, able to ward off winter colds.

9 April

Acacia cognata

If you want some foliage interest in your garden, a clutch of *Acacia cognata* 'Limelight', with its soft weeping leaves, will form a living sculpture in any frost-free garden. The nursery that bred this useful architectural plant released its cousin, *A. cognata* 'Curvaceous', in 2008. This variety bears very dense, but soft and gentle, growth, creating a voluptuous, billowing shape before long. Once established it is drought-tolerant and just about maintenance-free: enough to cheer even the gloomiest winter's day!

The soft form of *Acacia cognata* 'Curvaceous', here at Susan and Graeme Jack's garden, Jack's Ridge, adds year-round structure.

10 April

Pumpkins

There are two ways to ascertain when your pumpkins and watermelons are ready to harvest. If you live in a cool climate the first frost will tell you, as it will cause the foliage to die; in warmer climates, the dying foliage will also tell you that the fruit will soon be ripe. If you gently tap the fruits, a hollow sound will also indicate that they are ready to harvest.

The 'Peace' rose

11 April

'Peace' rose

The greatly loved 'Peace' rose was created by the Meilland family between 1935 and 1939, at their nursery near Lyons in the south of France. It is a hybrid tea rose, formally known as *Rosa* 'Mme A Meilland', and is pale yellow flushed with pink. Few plants have such a charming, and moving, tale associated with their name: a story well known through books such as Antonia Ridge's 1965 *For the Love of a Rose*. When rosarian François Meilland saw that World War II was inevitable, and imminent, he sent cuttings of the rose to horticultural colleagues around the world, who propagated it, and therefore protected it. The name 'Peace' was suggested by Field Marshal Alan Brooke, to whom Meilland wrote at the end of the war, requesting that Brooke give his name to the rose. 'Peace' was announced to the gardening world in the United States on 29 April 1945, the day on which Berlin fell.

12 April

Onions

If you're organised, and disciplined, in caring for your garden beds, you will have weeded, cut back, added aged manure to replenish the soil, and mulched well. You're ready to start again: it's time to plant winter vegetables. Sow onions now—red, brown or white—while the ground is still warm; they'll grow through winter, for final harvesting when the warm months return. Onions don't need to be confined to the vegie garden; weave the decorative plants, with their rich-green foliage topped with cream, or purple, globe-like inflorescences, through flower borders. They also look smart planted in straight rows, or as an edging plant.

13 April

Soil pH

Every gardener has heard the term 'pH', and many understand its meaning and relevance to the success of any garden. But most would not know that the term stands for 'power of hydrogen' and that it was first introduced in 1909 by a Danish chemist as the measure of acidity of a solution.

Azaleas, here at the Humble Administrator's Garden, in China, love acid soil.

Soil pH is the measure—from 1 to 14—of its acidity or alkalinity. A low soil pH indicates an acidic soil, suitable for plants such as camellias, azaleas and magnolias. A high pH indicates an alkaline soil, preferred by lavenders. Lawn grasses like a neutral pH. Although it is difficult to turn an alkaline soil acidic, an acidic soil can be made more alkaline by the addition of garden lime. In fact, while a neutral pH is best for most plants, many will thrive in either acidic or alkaline soil; more crucial than the pH is that they receive regular and correct fertilising and watering.

It is possible to determine the pH and mineral content of your soil with a home soil-testing kit, bought from your local nursery, or you can send a soil sample to the soil-testing service at the Department of Primary Industries in your state or territory. Once you know the balance of nitrogen, phosphorus and potassium in your soil—all vital minerals for plant health—you can fertilise accordingly. It is important to remember that soil make-up can vary in different parts of a garden—particularly a large garden—so it is necessary to take samples from several areas.

14 April

Broccoli

Broccoli is among the most rewarding plants of the brassica genus, part of the mustard family, which includes Brussels sprouts and cabbages. A leaf vegetable, broccoli is traditionally planted in autumn for early winter harvesting, although 'Green Dragon' can be harvested through summer. Watch out for the tiny pale-green larvae of the white cabbage moth; before they multiply and the moths rise in clouds from your brassicas, combat them with Dipel or Success.

Harvest the small heads of broccoli that appear for months, if you don't allow flowers to form. Broccoli is delicious chopped, lightly sautéed in olive oil, with a knob of butter, a touch of finely chopped chilli and crushed garlic. I like to add some chopped anchovies, too.

15 April

Mount Wilson

Simply wandering the lanes that wind through the tiny hamlet of Mount Wilson, in New South Wales, and peering over established hedges into gardens replete with century-old exotic trees, is exhilarating. During most months of the year log fires send swirling, scented smoke into the cool mountain air to shroud the area in a romantic atmosphere.

Above and previous pages: Merry Garth is glorious through each season.

The rich-red basalt soil of this hamlet, a volcanic knoll 1500 metres above sea level, in the Blue Mountains, supports some of Australia's loveliest gardens. One of these is Merry Garth. Owners Keith and Elizabeth Raines are plant collectors who propagate their treasures to sell in their excellent nursery. While the garden relies upon gentle colours, this month, Mollis and Ghent azaleas will be a blaze of scented oranges and yellows, illuminating the mists that swirl through the tall trees nearby.

The first area that visitors come to in this exciting garden is the Winter Garden, an early flowering rainforest, with an understorey of scented rhododendrons and azaleas. The rare *Enkianthus deflexus*, a small tree that bears pink-veined, cream flowers, is underplanted in tiers, with several cultivars of bleeding heart, as well as snowbells, the dwarf white wood lily and, in spring, the delicate blue wood anemone. Elsewhere, rare trout lilies (*Erythronium californicum* 'White Beauty'), with their white, mottled foliage, grow beneath a collection of magnolias.

On the way to the woodland walk are the difficult *Daphne genkwa* and the prostrate broom (*Cytisus × kewensis*), a mass of cream, scented, pea-shaped flowers. In the woodland, the ground cover *Sanguisorba obtusa* sends up its crimson plumes in summer, and rhododendrons fill the air with a heavenly lemon scent. In the rainforest walk, giant coast banksias jostle with possumwoods and giant blackwoods. And in a further woodland walk, which leads back to the front of the garden, the camellias 'Julia Hamiter' and 'Mary Phoebe Taylor' crowd together with more rhododendrons and the delicate red foliage of Japanese maples. Underfoot are drifts of tiny, scented dwarf daffodils. In early September, mauve and yellow crocuses, along with clumps of dainty, nodding snowdrops, illuminate the shaded area, and camellias, rhododendrons and early daffodils burst into flower.

16 April

Stone troughs

Some gardeners, like me, are content to plant their vegies in polystyrene fruit boxes, which the local fruit shop is more than happy to give away. These boxes appeal to me because they can be moved about—out of the way of teenage boys kicking footballs—and following the path of the sun. However, if you don't like the look of them, or you think visitors may disapprove, it is easy to make smart faux-stone troughs—though not without a certain amount of mess!

Stone troughs, 'faux' or otherwise, are perfect for alpine species and bulbs.

Combine two buckets each of coarse sand and composted pine bark or peat, one bucket of cement mix and one cup of coloured oxide. A cement mixer is ideal for this, although it can also be successfully mixed by hand. Slowly add water until the consistency of the mix is firm with just a little water dripping out when squeezed into a ball. Cover a pile of wet sand with the mix—or use a polystyrene box as a template—to create the desired size and shape of the finished trough. Use a hose to punch drainage holes in the base, while it's still wet. Allow the trough to dry, and then remove it from the template of sand, or break away the polystyrene box. It takes just a little time and practice to achieve the look of a master Italian stonemason.

17 April

Edible ferns

Did you know that some ferns are edible? New Zealand's Maori people value the diminutive hen and chicken fern (*Asplenium bulbiferum*) for its young shoots, which taste like asparagus.

18 April

Lawns

Some gardeners feel that they have failed if their lawn browns off in winter, which occurs with warm-climate, perennial, running species. To combat browning, try oversowing the lawn, in autumn, with a cool-climate grass, which will remain green in winter. A combination of grass varieties, such as blue and green couch together, can suit some climates and growing conditions.

19 April

Quince

There are plenty of quinces in the markets now, and they are cheap. It's easy to slow-bake this rather ugly fruit into ruby-red, richly flavoured quarters, to be enjoyed with savoury or sweet dishes. Baked quinces last for months, and, sealed in plastic tubs, they freeze well, too. Leave a bowl on your kitchen bench for a gorgeous fragrance to fill the house. (They were once placed on the top of wardrobes to alleviate musty smells.) If you live in a cold climate, you can enjoy the elegant pink blossom of the quince tree; the flowers emerge from among beautiful pale-green leaves in early spring. Be alert for the pear and cherry slug, however, just as you watch for this pest on your pear and apple trees.

20 April

A quiet vignette—the stone basin located near the tea house in Kyoto's Saiho-ji (Moss Temple) is used for washing hands.

21 April

Autumn colours

With the fall in temperatures comes the excitement of autumn performances in the garden, with a range of deciduous trees available to provide plenty of drama. Even the most humble tree species can become stars in autumn, as their foliage takes on fiery colours. Plants' autumn tones depend upon the genetic make-up of the particular species, the rainfall and hours of sunlight received, and the temperatures experienced during the autumn season, when plants store sugars and available nutrients. Cold nights are required for the development of the deepest colours. The production of green chlorophyll falls as the nights become longer, and other compounds, which produce the yellows, golds and reds, increase, assisted by the higher sugar levels in the leaves. Reds and purples are encouraged by the antioxidant anthocyanins; the yellows are derived from carotenoids.

Among the best autumn performers are the Persian ironwood (*Parrotia persica*), a small spreading tree that reaches to about 4 metres: its leaves turn yellow, gold and orange at the first hint that the end of summer is near. The graceful North American snowdrop tree (*Halesia monticolor*) follows, its leaves turning pink and red. Next, fiery-red Canadian maples accompany paperbark maples; along with the leaves, their peeling, vibrant bark should ensure that they have a place in any garden. The filigreed leaves of Japanese maples flutter in the autumn breezes, providing essential contrast in texture and captivating plays in light and shadow. The claret ash (*Fraxinus angustifolia* 'Raywood') becomes a mass of deep-purple leaves, and the dawn redwoods (*Metasequoia glyptostroboides*), among the few deciduous conifers, colour a rust red. Tupelos (*Nyssa sinensis* and *N. sylvatica*) light up in a range of pinks and reds, and tulip trees turn yellow, along with birches.

22 April

Asparagus

Have you prepared your asparagus bed yet? Asparagus has long seemed to me to be a somewhat mysterious vegetable, with its exacting cultivation needs, and my visits to several large country gardens that boast century-old asparagus beds have only added to its intrigue. Asparagus grows best in temperate to cold climates, but it loves the sun. Plant the crowns, in autumn or early winter, where they can receive perfect drainage, and remain undisturbed for decades. Grow two plants for each member of your family.

The spears that we all love so much—poached and served with butter, pepper, salt and a shaving of parmesan—are the emerging shoots of the ferny leaves. Therefore, don't be too greedy too soon: it is important to allow your asparagus to grow fully in the first year, after which you should leave some spears to develop feathery heads to support the following year's harvest.

Lift established clumps in mid-winter and divide them by cutting back, turning over and teasing apart the crown. Replant with the crown at soil level. Asparagus is a heavy feeder, but is very long-lived if cherished.

23 April

Walnut trees

If you have walnut trees in your garden, you will be looking forward to harvesting the delicious nuts soon. Native to southern Europe, the Indian subcontinent and China, walnut trees bear aromatic leaves and pale-grey bark, and are often twisted charmingly, forming a sculptural shape. They are beautiful trees for a large garden. The wood is coveted for cabinet-making, while the walnut husks are used in dyeing: you need to wear gloves, therefore, when gathering up your harvest.

24 April

A mown path through a meadow garden can be most effective.

Meadows

It's time to mow the meadow—before the spring bulbs start to emerge. That is, if you have a garden large enough to incorporate a wildflower meadow. This romantic space—a generous expanse of native flowers, grasses and flowering bulbs—can connect the formal section of a garden with its more natural, or wild, edges: a winding, mown path through the meadow may help to accomplish this. The easiest way to achieve such insouciance is with a collection of flowering bulbs that will start to bloom in mid winter and continue into early summer. This style of gardening, which has become fashionable once again, is not, however, maintenance-free. (And in many parts of the country you need to be conscious of snakes.)

25 April

Anzac Day

Today is Anzac Day, when we honour Australian and New Zealand soldiers who have died in the wars of the past century. It is also the time to sow seeds of the red Flanders poppy (*Papaver rhoeas*), also known as the field poppy, which self-seeds so evocatively throughout much of Europe. It is a symbol of the soldiers of World War I who fell on the battlefields of northern France, where it carpets the ground in spring. The poppy does not flourish so prolifically in this country; it demands well-drained soil and full sun, and flowers in November. (On Remembrance Day, the eleventh day of the eleventh month, Australians join others around the world in wearing this red poppy as a mark of respect to fallen soldiers in all wars. This is the day, in 1918, when the guns

The red poppy is a symbol of the sacrifice of fallen soldiers.

on the Western Front fell silent and the Armistice came into force, bringing World War I to an end.)

26 April

The foxtail lily

Some plants seem to thrive in the most inhospitable of places. Take the foxtail lily (*Eremurus* spp.). Several species grow wild on Iran's high plateau, standing tall and straight—and covered in lilac or pink star-like flowers—against icy winds and snow. The lily is said to tolerate a variety of climates, from warm temperate to cold, but I find that it hates humidity—which makes sense when you consider where it grows naturally.

27 April

Thomas Church

The American landscaper Thomas Dolliver Church was born on this day in 1902, in Boston. He is best remembered, perhaps, for coining the phrase 'Gardens are for people', the title of his first book, published in 1955. In it, he emphasised the principles central to his garden designs: unity, function, simplicity and scale. His most renowned, and much-photographed, commission, the El Novillero garden at Sonoma, California, was constructed between 1947 and 1949, and is symbolic of a pared-down style that placed greatest importance on the relationship between the garden and house and the people who were to enjoy them—along with the suitability of the design to its setting.

28 April

Isfahan

Isfahan, in central Iran, is a place to dream about. Designated the Safavid capital in 1597 by Shah Abbas, this garden city—with its streets and parks shaded by pink-flowering cercis trees and almond blossom—has been the romantic muse of rulers, writers, artists and travellers for centuries. At the heart of the city is the enormous Maydan-e-shah (Imperial Square), considered one of the architectural marvels of the world, which contains cooling water features, arcades of shops, a cavernous bazaar and magnificent mosques. The majestic gateway to the Shah Mosque leads off the square, while the mosque itself—with its intricately patterned tiles, many with a botanical motif, that cover the interior walls and the large dome—is turned on an angle, towards Mecca. As Robert Byron wrote in 1937, in *The Road to Oxiana*, 'The beauty of Isfahan steals on the mind unawares … Before you know how, Isfahan has become indelible, has insinuated its image into that gallery of places which everyone privately treasures'.

29 April

Colour combining

I love playing with colour combinations. Each year, at the end of April, I plant out hundreds of burgundy tulips in my front garden. They flower through August in tandem with the *Magnolia × soulangiana*, which blooms

The sunset colours of *Canna* 'Tropicanna', together with black taro (*Colocasia esculenta* 'Black Magic')

in a lighter pink of the same tone. Pink salvias flower in August as well, and their lime-green leaves unfurl. It is a beautiful combination and adds great excitement to the garden for several weeks in late winter.

My colours for summer are hot, however, with the orange flowers of easy-to-please cannas blooming with the strappy, cerise foliage of cordylines, all toned down by the black leaves of taros.

30 April

Miss Fotheringham's slice

This recipe for my favourite slice graces my Year 8 home science cookbook, in my childhood handwriting. I still make it regularly, several decades after my first attempt, and love the way it fills the house with a caramel smell as it bakes.

Caramel walnut slice

FOR THE BISCUIT BASE
90 g unsalted butter
1 cup brown sugar
1 egg
1 cup self-raising flour, sifted with pinch salt
½ cup mixed fruit, chopped
½ cup dates, chopped
¼ cup walnuts, chopped
1 teaspoon vanilla essence

FOR THE TOPPING
2 tablespoons brown sugar
1 tablespoon milk
1 cup icing sugar, sifted
1 teaspoon vanilla essence

Grease a scone tray. Preheat oven to 180°C. Cream butter and sugar together, add egg and beat well. Add vanilla essence. Fold in flour and salt, then fruit and nuts. Spread the mixture evenly onto tray. Bake for 20–30 minutes, or until cake is light brown. It will still be soft, but will harden as it cools. When cool, cut into fingers or squares.

For the topping, melt sugar with milk and vanilla essence in a saucepan and stir in icing sugar. Spread quickly onto slice while topping is warm.

May

1 May

Paradise Plants

The camellias are in bloom. To feast your eyes on a huge range, visit Paradise Plants, the 10-hectare garden and nursery at Kulnura, an hour's drive north of Sydney, which is open to the public on the first weekend in May each year. Enjoy the *sasanqua* camellias, thrill to the vibrant foliage colours of hundreds of exotic trees, and drink in the scent of the flush of autumn roses. The garden also includes magnolias, michelias and gordonias, many of which have been sourced on the owners' trips to wild and beautiful parts of south-west China. There are guided tours, and the New South Wales Camellia Research Society is always on hand with displays of this genus, and to identify your treasures.

2 May

Lilly pillies

What's easy to please, can be used as a shade tree or clipped into a hedge or a smart topiary, and produces powder puffs of white, nectar-laden blossom that attracts the birds and the bees, as well as gorgeous red berries that you can eat in a variety of ways? It is the riberry (*Syzygium luehmannii*), of course, part of the lilly pilly genus: a rainforest tree that can reach 30 metres in its natural environment, but can also be clipped regularly, which will encourage glossy, pink tips. Perhaps the best known of bush food plants, the riberry can be made into jams, jellies, sauces and glazes, and can be poached to use with meats.

The lilly pillies are blooming now—and most bear fruit and flowers at the same time. They have smooth, glossy leaves that have bronze, pink, cerise or lime-green tips when young. They are members of the Myrtaceae family, which also includes callistemons, eucalypts and melaleucas, and belong to the *Syzygium*, *Acmena* and *Waterhousia* genera (which are so closely related that they are now considered by some botanists to all belong to the genus *Syzygium*). Lilly pillies will tolerate a range of soils; they love the sun but will cope with shade; and there are varieties to suit every climate, any aspect and most situations.

Make sure you buy a psyllid-resistant variety of lilly pilly. Among these, *S.* 'Cascade' copes well with coastal situations. *S.* 'Winter Lights' has brilliant-red new foliage and fluffy, white flowers followed by purple fruits: it will grow to between 3 and 5 metres in height. There are several small-growing varieties available, including *S. australe* 'Aussie Compact', and the dwarf *S. australe* 'Tiny Trev', which has small, tightly packed leaves and makes a great low hedge: use it as you would box. Its new growth is bronze, making it a smart companion for a second hedge of the low-growing *Pittosporum* 'Tom Thumb', with its burgundy foliage.

There are fifteen species in the *Acmena* genus, all evergreen rainforest trees native to Australia and New Guinea. They have glossy, smooth-edged leaves and bear fluffy, white flowers in panicles at the ends of their branches. *A. smithii* 'Sublime' has stunning lime-green foliage, and is psyllid-resistant; it is also compact-growing, making it ideal for clipping into topiary or hedges: you might imagine it restraining a swathe of hot-pink tulips or pink salvias. More tolerant of cool climates, and popular for hedges in Melbourne, *Waterhousia floribunda* has glossy, green leaves and white or pink powder-puff flowers, followed by gorgeous red berries.

3 May

Composting

The first week of May is International Composting Awareness Week (www .compostweek.com.au), which celebrates the virtues of composting. We all know that great gardens begin with great soil. Soil is a living community, full of micro-organisms and animals that rely for their nutrition upon the organic matter in, or on, the soil. Soil particles are held together by fine strands of fungus and by secretions produced by countless bacteria. Compost and humus improve soil structure and its ability to hold moisture and take up nutrients, and the practice of composting garden and kitchen waste reduces greenhouse gas emissions and landfill, with all their associated problems.

Almost anything can be composted, except meat and milk products (and many organic gardeners won't add paper with coloured inks to their compost pile). If you live in a small city block you will want a closed compost bin to ensure that vermin don't make themselves at home. I like the barrel types best and believe you need two: one nicely mature and one 'on the go'. If you live on country hectares you will have room for a three-bale arrangement (of separate wooden compartments housing material in varying stages of decomposition) constructed well away from the house.

4 May

Camellia mite

Now that the camellia season is in full swing, watch out for camellia mite, which can turn those deep-green leaves that we love to an unappealing silver or brown, and can eventually cause the tree to defoliate and die. The microscopic mites, which thrive in dry conditions, can cause fine webbing: water the leaves to increase humidity or spray the surface and underside of the leaves with Natrasoap or Eco-Neem.

5 May

Ballarat Botanic Gardens

May I paraphrase an admonition from the English gardener and writer Vita Sackville-West? If you've never been to Ballarat, please visit immediately. Well, soon, at least, because it's a beautiful city, of wide streets lined with majestic trees that are more than a century old. Gold was discovered in the nearby village of Clunes in 1851, and as a result of the ensuing wealth, Ballarat boasts a heritage of magnificent public and private buildings, as well as wonderful parks, public gardens and street plantings.

In many provincial Victorian towns, part of the legacy of the gold rush was the establishment of important botanical gardens, and in Ballarat a council-run competition to design the city's gardens was won by Messrs Wright and Armstrong in 1858. Set on Lake Wendouree, the gardens are an example of nineteenth-century gardenesque style, with its great emphasis on the placement of individual trees.

This was a time when an energetic plant exchange took place between the botanic gardens of the world, and Ferdinand von Mueller, first director of Melbourne's Royal Botanic Gardens, supplied many specimens to Ballarat, including the conifers he hoped would seed a forestry industry. Among them

The succulent garden at Ballarat's Botanic Gardens

were Queensland's bunya pine (*Araucaria bidwillii*), its huge cones a source of food for Aboriginal people; the Himalayan cedar (*Cedrus deodara*); and a Scotch pine (*Pinus sylvestris*), now some 20 metres in height. They all remain magnificent trees. There is also a Scotch elm (*Ulmus glabra* 'Exoniensis'), planted in 1905 and now 16 metres tall, along with the rare New Zealand puriri (*Vitex lucens*), an evergreen which reaches 15 metres, and bears sprays of pink flowers in spring.

Central to the gardens is an avenue—more than a kilometre long—of *Sequoiadendron giganteum*, commonly known as wellingtonias. Planted in 1871, this avenue leads from a war memorial, at one end, to the site of a former zoo, where exotic animals were once collected by one of the acclimatisation societies that were part of nineteenth-century colonial life.

6 May

Gardenia pruning

In warm, temperate climates, it's time to prune your gardenias if you want wonderful scented displays in time for Christmas. While this genus of around 300 species—native to Africa and Asia—is thirsty, and so is not,

Fertilise gardenias as winter approaches to ensure a scented summer display.

perhaps, your first choice in these days of water restrictions, there are few other blooms that can boast such a divine scent. Just one gardenia in a vase will fill a room with fragrance. Use the different species for various landscape applications: the prostrate *G. radicans* is useful for planting at the front of a border, or to cascade down a retaining wall. *G. augusta*, native to China and Japan, has large, glossy, deep-green foliage, while its offspring, 'Florida', grows to about 1 metre tall and has double flowers from spring, through to the end of autumn. 'Grandiflora' has larger leaves and blooms, while 'Magnifica' has the largest flowers of all.

Gardenias love basking in the sun, and enjoy a good drink; they also like a feed, so, during the flowering season, apply a general garden fertiliser each fortnight, after watering.

7 May

Design thoughts

No matter how small your garden, it will benefit from the inclusion of vistas and focal points. When considering such elements of design, remember that strong bright colours 'stop' the eye, while light colours and fine foliage draw it to a focal point, or into the distance, creating a sense of space. Among the Australian native species you might consider to extend the garden are the paperbarks (*Melaleuca incana*, *M. styphelioides* and *M. armillaris*), with their fine, soft foliage and cream blossom. The clouds of dreamy-blue flowers provided by the Californian lilacs (*Ceanothus impressus* and *C. edwardii*), the mass, tone and gentle colour of almond and pear blossom, and the fine foliage of the Cape snowbush (*Eriocephalus africanus*) can create a line of sight towards a vista. You might add a piece of sculpture at the end of such a view: think of a huge apple carved from local stone at the end of a mown path through an orchard, for instance.

An above-ground garden makes harvesting and tending your flowers and vegetables easier.

8 May

Above-ground gardens

Do you want a vegie patch, but don't want to up-end your garden, or fill in your swimming pool or water feature? The Brisbane-based company Birdies Garden Products (www.birdiesgardenproducts.com.au) has come up with a range of corrugated iron 'bays' in a variety of sizes that are simply placed on the lawn, or even on concrete, filled with soil, and planted up. While pots, polystyrene boxes and 'grow bags' can also make good receptacles for vegetables and herbs, some—like potatoes and tall-growing tomato varieties—need deeper soil. These waist-height garden beds are also good for those who move house regularly, or for those who can't bend to garden.

9 May

Deciduous creepers

It will soon be time to prune back those gorgeous creepers that add mellow gravitas to old walls, and make the shabbiest fence look smart. Boston ivy (*Parthenocissus tricuspidata*) and Virginia Creeper (*P. quinquefolia*) are two of the best, and safest, creepers. If you have allowed them to cling to your house, cut them away from windows, and remove from guttering. Today, however, just enjoy the wonderful autumn yellows, oranges and reds.

10 May

Hips and berries

There is probably no month of the year when you can't find something to pick from your garden to decorate the house. While spring and summer offer an endless variety of scented and colourful blooms for the vase, autumn, and even winter, provide fruits, hips, berries, fiery-toned leaves and interesting stems that can be cut to create a warm sense of harvest abundance. Many rose species develop fascinating hips; viburnums hold coloured berries through much of autumn and winter; crab-apples bear fruit on graceful branches; and the turning colours of many deciduous trees allow you to pay tribute to the joy of the season.

11 May

Mother's Day

Mother's Day falls on the second Sunday in May; it is, of course, the day when families get together, in gardens and parks around the country, to honour their mothers. It is also the day on which you should pick your olives!

12 May

Citrus

If you enjoy a juicy orange, picked warm from your own tree in mid-winter, it's time to think about citrus. Citruses fulfil all the criteria of a good garden plant: they are edible, beautiful, fragrant, and can be used in many different ways, from hedging and feature shrubs, to smart potted specimens. Citruses are not maintenance-free, however, and, if you want plenty of sweet, juicy fruit, a certain amount of care is needed.

Attack by sucking insects, which can lead to unsightly sooty mould, can be countered by early applications of an organic horticultural oil such as eco-oil. And watch out for bronze orange bugs, a few of which may still be appearing. Perhaps more appropriately known as stink bugs, these unpleasant creatures cause the flesh of the fruit to go brown. The eggs will be on the trees now, so it is time to prevent them from hatching and developing by spraying fortnightly with eco-oil: this will smother the eggs. If you leave it too late and the bugs appear in summer, you will need to use Confidor—being very careful to protect your eyes, as they can spray a dangerous poison. Yellowing leaves on citrus indicate that the plant is deficient in iron. Counter this by spraying with a solution of iron chelates on the foliage, or, for a large tree, drenching the soil with it. To avoid thick skins and sour, dry fruit, water deeply at fruiting time; but citruses hate being waterlogged, which will cause leaves to drop, and uneven watering can cause fruit drop.

You can prevent many problems by keeping the plants healthy. Citruses are greedy, so feed them in early autumn, after harvest and again in late spring. To make the busy gardener's life easier, Yates has released a specially formulated Dynamic Lifter for fruit and citrus: it contains all the necessary nutrients, including trace elements, in the correct balance, to keep fruit succulent. Sprinkle it around the drip line once you've watered, and water again afterwards.

Remove young fruit in the first three years of a citrus's life to encourage a strong plant, and then thin out heavy crops to ensure better quality fruit. Citruses don't need much pruning. You may want to trim the base of the shrub to keep branches, and fruit, clear of the soil, or prune just to keep them in shape, cutting out any misshapen, crowding or crossing branches.

A civic garden of broderie in the ancient French town of Albi

13 May

Knots and parterres

If you love intricate patterns, and enjoy hours of plotting and planning, you might consider including a knot garden, or the larger parterre, in your garden. Knot and parterre gardens (the terms are often interchangeable) have been part of garden design in many different cultures for hundreds of years. These garden styles served a functional purpose in medieval times, when low hedging—often of different species—was used to separate different medicinal herbs. Knots and parterres formed part of the decorative aesthetic of the Italian Renaissance and of the aristocratic gardens of France, where *parterres de broderie* were status symbols. In Tudor and Elizabethan gardens, parterres often created a mediating space between the house and the farmland or natural landscape beyond. As garden-making takes on a renewed importance in the twenty-first century, the knot and parterre—large or small—is once again often central to a landscape plan.

The beauty of this garden feature (which is best viewed from a high point so that the design can be fully appreciated) is firstly derived from its intricate shape, drawn with a variety of species, but most commonly with box. The structure alone takes on different moods as seasons change, often picked out in frost or snow in cold climates in winter; in fresh, new spring growth; and in deep-green, sharply crisp outlines in summer. The segments and shapes can be in-filled with spring-flowering bulbs, or herbs in summer, or vegetables or flowers. The parterre can house topiary or tripods, and can be the design solution for a difficult site. It can be as complicated, or as restrained, as is the garden maker's personal taste; I suspect, however, that the knot or parterre garden will never be low-maintenance.

At the centre of the beautifully laid out and maintained Knot Garden at Great Fosters, England, is a sundial once owned by the English admiral Sir Francis Drake.

14 May

Pitcher plants

Surely the strangest of all the species in the botanical world are the carnivorous plants, among them the pitcher plants (*Nepenthes* spp.), native to the jungles of Borneo. They bear inconspicuous flowers, but develop large, often pendulous, 'pitchers' on their leaves, in shades of rust and burgundy. While insects are their usual prey, rats, and even monkeys, who have wandered into these cavities, perhaps to drink from the water held there, have been devoured. A genus of some seventy species, pitcher plants love the humidity of tropical regions, and moist, fertile soil.

15 May

Villa Reale

It is late spring in the Northern Hemisphere, and Italy's gardens will be at their peak—lush and green. Villa Reale, located in the village of Marlia, in Tuscany, houses one of the world's first green theatres. Named the Garden Theatre, it was built in 1652, and is 24 metres deep. Created from hedges of yew, into which windows have been cut, the theatre houses stone seats arranged in a semicircle.

The extensive grounds at Villa Reale contain two very different gardens: a wild area that is part of a parkland of ancient trees, and a more formal area of orangeries and parterres bordered with magnolias that are pruned into pillars and which frame views to the surrounding mountains. This section of the garden includes a wonderful water theatre: a large semicircular pool surrounded by a stone balustrade adorned with statues of gods and tubs of flowers.

If you are ever fortunate enough to visit the region, spend several days in Lucca, among the most beautiful of all Italian towns, laid out in the Middle Ages to a Roman street plan, and surrounded by a remarkable perimeter wall. Wander through the Piazza Amfiteatro, Piazza San Michele and Piazza Grande. Explore the ramparts, and the elegant shops, and enjoy coffee in the beautiful Antico Café in Via Fillunga. But do watch out for the very smartly dressed cycling grandmothers!

16 May

Callistemons

You would think that *Callistemon salignus* 'Great Balls of Fire' would flower in hot colours, wouldn't you? Well, you would be right. This dwarf bottlebrush blooms in hot-pink inflorescences, and the new foliage is red. Like many of our native plants, the callistemons will be in full bloom now, attracting a chorus of birds, many of which are also brilliantly coloured. The aptly named scarlet bottlebrush (*C. citrinus*) is the parent of many cultivars, including 'Reeves Pink', 'White Anzac' and 'Mauve Mist'. *C. viminalis* 'Harkness', which grows to about 4.5 metres, is easy-going and not fussy about its growing conditions. They all make great hedges, if you prune them from the start to create a dense form, while the taller growing callistemons can be carefully pruned into elegant trees. Callistemons also look stunning combined with grevilleas. And the native birds love them: watch out for the flash of red and blue that darts past your face. It will be a crimson rosella, drunk with joy as it feasts on the indigenous species that are in full flower through most of winter, and on, into spring.

17 May

Writer Edith Wharton's house, The Mount, in the Berkshires in the United States

The Mount

The term 'The Gilded Age', which came from the 1873 satirical novel of the same name by Mark Twain and Charles Dudley Warner, initially referred to the corruption and excesses of political and social life in the United States during the nineteenth century. Nowadays, the term is used to describe the age of privilege among the American moneyed classes of the nineteenth and early twentieth centuries, and is not always afforded a pejorative meaning: it often refers to the period in which the glorious, grand gardens in the hills to the west of New York and Boston were laid out. Such gardens included Edith Wharton's The Mount, and Naumkeag, created for the Choate family, both in the beautiful Berkshires, west of Boston.

18 May

Many towns and villages throughout Australia lost young men during World War I: at Chudleigh, in northern Tasmania, Lombardy poplars (*Populus nigra*) were planted in their honour, one to commemorate each young life sacrificed.

19 May

Wiring wisteria

As we are blessed, in this country, with many clear, blue-sky days, even in the coldest months, winter is a great time to tidy the hard surfaces in the garden. This includes painting fences, screens and lattices. You will perhaps have trained your wisteria on stand-alone wires so that this vigorous climber will not hoist itself up on your woodwork. If so, once the vine is bare, you can lay the entire wire frame on the ground, with wisteria attached, to allow you to paint, or to repair woodwork or point work behind it. Deciduous trees such as magnolias, which can be espaliered on flat surfaces, can be laid down in the same way to allow maintenance to take place.

Opposite: The beautiful water expanses at Longstock are edged with bog garden species.

Longstock gardens

Among the loveliest water gardens you will find anywhere in the world are those at Longstock Gardens (www.longstockpark.co.uk), in the English county of Hampshire. Comprising several small islands connected by bridges, these serene gardens contain a collection of lush bog species and statuesque examples of such damp-loving trees as swamp cypress. There is no other word to describe them: these gardens are simply gorgeous.

21 May

Winter is never gloomy when beauties like *Camellia sasanqua* 'Mine-no-yuki' bloom.

Camellias

Who said winter was a dull season? It can't have been a gardener, for this is the month when camellias are at their peak. They started in February with the *sasanqua* species, but are still in full bloom through much of winter, as beautiful feature trees, dense hedges and even ground covers. The sasanquas will still be flowering, but it is the japonicas that shout the loudest this month. The 'Cup of Beauty' in my garden is covered in elegant blush-pink double blooms that are splashed with crushed raspberry—and it will continue flowering into spring.

Camellia gigantocarpa flowers in autumn and winter and, in addition, boasts wonderful bark; *C. yunnanensis* grows to about 4 metres, and flowers through winter.

In frosty climates, plant camellias—particularly the white-flowering varieties—in a position where the dawn sun will not burn the blooms, which may be dusted with dew. Give camellias a good deep soaking at least once a week. And keep an eye out for notices of the several camellia shows being held around the country.

22 May

Chelsea Flower Show

The annual Chelsea Flower Show, which has been staged in London by the Royal Horticultural Society since 1913, is a mecca for gardeners: the four-day event attracts some 160 000 visitors. It is held over the last week of May.

There are some 600 exhibitors at Chelsea; it takes 800 people almost a month to construct the show. Judging of the exhibits and the show gardens is the culmination of months of presentations, meticulous planning, devoted hard work, sacrifice and hundreds of thousands of sponsors' dollars. In the grand pavilion—the size of three rugby fields—over 100 floral exhibitors display an extraordinary range of horticultural bravura.

Chelsea is about trends and fashion, about inspiration and information, about pushing botanical boundaries and mixing the possible with the fantastic. It is not surprising that the show is emotion-charged: the designers of the show gardens are stars, and, in a country that erupts into garden mania for the few warm months of the year, they are celebrities.

23 May

Botanical names

The Swedish botanist, physician and zoologist Carl Linnaeus was born on this day in 1707. He is celebrated for devising the botanical nomenclature that remains the common language of horticulturalists all over the world. His system of grouping and naming the characteristics of plants means that all plants can be recognised and understood: essential when the common name for a plant differs between countries.

In the Linnaeus system each plant is given two names which come after the family name. The first name is the genus, and groups plants with similar characteristics together. (Sometimes genera are named after explorers or botanists; for example, the *Banksia* is named after the amateur botanist Joseph Banks.) The second name is the species and describes particular idiosyncrasies of a plant within a genus. For example, the botanical name *Parthenocissus tricuspidata* indicates that the leaves of this creeping vine are three-lobed.

Cultivated varieties, or cultivars, are developed from a particular species, and this name is written after the genus and species, enclosed in inverted commas.

24 May

Catherine Hamlin

The Australian gynaecologist Dr Catherine Hamlin, AC, and her husband, Dr Reg Hamlin, OAM, opened their Fistula Hospital, in Addis Ababa, Ethiopia, on this day in 1975. Catherine Hamlin arrived in Addis Ababa in 1959 with her husband and six-year-old son, Richard, and has since devoted her life to helping Ethiopian women who have suffered devastating injuries through obstructed and prolonged childbirth: her work is documented in the 2007 film *A Walk to Beautiful*.

Catherine was a student at Frensham, a girls school at Mittagong, in New South Wales, from 1936 to 1940. Like many who attended the school, she remembers the influence of the charismatic founder and headmistress, Winifred West, for whom the garden provided the canvas upon which philosophies for living and for community service could be written. 'Miss West was a great influence on my life and I am sure the beautiful garden she created at Frensham gave me a love of flowers and lawns and trees,' Catherine told me. 'I have tried to create a beautiful garden around our hospital.'

25 May

What is a weed?

The American philosopher, orator and writer Ralph Waldo Emerson was born in Boston on this day in 1803. He was a leader in the transcendentalist movement in the early nineteenth century, but he is perhaps most important to gardeners for his definition, given during a lecture in 1878, of a weed as 'a plant whose virtues have not yet been discovered'. Others will say that a weed is any plant growing in the wrong place. So, a mass of violets growing, as intended, as a mono-culture to provide a ground cover in a woodland setting may be just what the designer intended, but, if planted in a mixed border, the tough little violet will soon take over from more gentle species. Any plant you don't want multiplying in your garden should be removed before it goes to seed: little and often is a useful adage here. Take to weeds early and your maintenance load will be lightened.

26 May

Kangaroo paws

It's time to attend to your paws: your kangaroo paws (*Anigozanthos* spp.). Use a complete plant food in spring and autumn for multiple flowers per stem. Kangaroo paws love lots of sunshine, and demand perfect drainage: grow them in pots if your soil is heavy. Cut them right back to the ground as soon as flowering is finished, in late summer, to encourage fresh new growth; they can then be divided. In mild climates they'll be flowering again by late spring. All varieties of 'paws' can suffer from fungal diseases which cause leaf blackening—the result of poor drainage, water or nutrient stress, or frost damage. Although they will survive harsh conditions of drought and nutrient deficiency, a regular moisture supply and moderate levels of fertiliser will result in taller, stronger spires of blooms. And be on guard: snails and slugs also love them.

The striking red and green kangaroo paw (*A. manglesii*) is named after the English amateur plant hunter and botanist Captain James Mangles, and is the state flower of Western Australia. The 'Bush Gem' series, bred by Angus Stewart, produces spectacular flower displays on shorter spikes: try the pink 'Bush Pearl' and the red 'Bush Inferno'. The gorgeous 'Bush Diamond' flowers white with a touch of pink.

27 May

Bellagio

The Italians have a noteworthy saying: 'In beautiful places you eat like a dog'. Sadly, I found this to be true at Bellagio, an exquisite little village perched on the eastern shore of glorious Lake Como, in Italy. From then on, I eschewed the rip-off restaurants that seemed to assume that tourists have no taste, and shopped instead at one of the excellent delicatessens, where I found delicious, fresh produce at amazingly good prices.

Bellagio boasts several excellent gardens, among them the Villa Melzi, just a short walk from the centre of the village, an extensive parkland garden of cold-climate trees, and the Rockefeller garden, created on several steep terraces that straddle both the east and west sides of the Bellagio peninsula that juts into Lake Como.

28 May

Heliconias

You'll need to garden in the tropical north of the country if you want to grow exotic beauties like the fabulous fishtail heliconia, sometimes called the hanging parrot (*Heliconia rostrata* 'Sexy Pink'). With its cascade of pink and apple-green bracts, it is just one in the vast collection of colourful genera from the Zingiberales group, which also contains the gingers. Plant fishtail heliconias en masse underneath shady trees and behind any brightly coloured foliage plants, or, perhaps, with an underplanting of vanda orchids. As with all plants in the wet tropics, they demand plenty of fertiliser to perform at their flamboyant best.

The flamboyant *Heliconia rostrata* 'Sexy Pink'

29 May

Old WesleyDale

One of Australia's most beautiful places is the Chudleigh Valley, which runs across northern Tasmania, from east to west. Flanked by mountains that are clothed in old-growth forests of native beech, stringybark, celerytop pine, satinwood and blackwood, and which feature pristine alpine meadows, the area is steeped in the history of both Aboriginal and European settlement. Old WesleyDale (www.oldwesleydaleheritage.com), part of the Native Plains, has been restored from a somewhat neglected garden that featured a few mature elm trees and an ancient orchard, and is now a cornucopia of flowers, fruit and vegetables, spreading over 2 hectares, with extraordinary views to the Western Tiers across fields and flood plains that were once fire-farmed by the local Pallitore people.

Kilometres of old, overgrown hawthorn hedges have been returned to working order. The art of hedge-laying, employed in the United Kingdom for more than 1000 years, involves making a partial cut in semi-mature wood. These cut stems or trunks are laid down, and secured in a variety of ways, depending upon the style and intended use of the hedge, and upon the heritage of the craftsman. Stakes are driven through to stabilise the plant material, and the top is bound. Suckers will emanate from the cuts, and within a few years a dense hedge, which will remain impenetrable for the next half-century, will have been created. Hedges are trimmed twice a year, in spring and late summer.

Amid the hard work and attention to historical detail that have been employed in the restoration of Old WesleyDale, a healthy sense of humour has been maintained. The lawn that rolls out from the farmhouse is skirted by a parade of marching elephants, clipped from a hedge of box honeysuckle (*Lonicera nitida*). The rear of the house protects a border of tall hollyhocks, frothy roses and wallflowers. From there, much of the back garden is given over to a potager of fruit and vegetables, beautifully designed around the existing orchard. Low trellises on which apples have been espaliered form 'step-over' hedges, and hurdles of woven willow separate the beds. Decorative tents and lattices of hazel prunings support climbing peas and beans.

30 May

Topiary

While winter is almost upon us clear, blue-sky days are not unusual, and provide the perfect opportunity for many outdoor chores. If topiary has a place in your garden, now is a good time for some clipping. Topiary features are perfect for small gardens, courtyards and balconies. Gardeners with a sense of humour employ topiary animals and birds to brighten gloomy corners where other plants refuse to thrive. It is fairly easy to create a template for such features with chicken wire. Cover the frame with climbing plants like ivy (*Hedera* spp.), Chinese star jasmine (*Trachelospermum jasminoides*) or the creeping wire vine (*Muehlenbeckia axillaris*), which is fast-growing and creates a fine, dense cover. Clip stray strands back to the frame as they appear.

For the more formally minded designer, the strong architectural shapes created by topiary tripods, obelisks and cones can be employed in gardens large and small. Use them as punctuation marks, to direct the garden traffic and to emphasise areas of your garden design. As with any clipped features in your garden, including espaliers, edges and hedges, clipping from the time of planting will ensure a more successful outcome.

Back by popular demand: the image of the topiary hedge of box honeysuckle at Old WesleyDale, at Chudleigh, Tasmania

31 May

Judith Wright

The poet Judith Arundell Wright, who was committed to conservation and to Aboriginal land rights, was born on this day in 1915, in Sydney. Her poetry captures perfectly an Australian sense of place; it speaks evocatively of the heat and the drought that are so much part of the Australian experience, and the colours, textures and forms of the Australian landscape.

June

1 June

Leeks

It's time to harvest your leeks. This mild-mannered member of the onion family, with its densely packed white end and deep-green top, is perfect added to a risotto, or braised, as an accompaniment to baked meats. If you haven't planted your onions yet, it's time to get busy. The broccoli are forming flower heads, ready for snapping off. Like all winter vegetables, the brassicas must be fed fortnightly with a liquid fertiliser, as they find the up-take of solid food more difficult when the soil is cold. And don't forget to feed your citrus, and to continue to protect it against the citrus leaf miner.

2 June

The oldest tree

There is some disagreement about which country is home to the world's oldest tree. Australia lays claim to the title, offering as evidence—although it is really a shrub—a King's lomatia (*Lomatia tasmanica*), a member of the Proteaceae family. In Sweden, a 9500-year-old spruce has been described using a radiocarbon dating method.

3 June

Tidy the shed

Along with servicing garden equipment such as lawn mowers, and sharpening and cleaning tools like secateurs, you may agree that winter is the time to tidy the garden shed. Put on the kettle, tune in the radio and set about finding a place for all those items you have been too busy to look after at other times of the year. One item I have been meaning to make for my own shed is a board for storing tools that I saw at someone else's garden. Simply take a large piece of plywood (you can frame it if you want it to be über-smart), hammer in nails for each item you want to hang on it, and then draw, in texta, around each tool as it hangs on its nail, to create its shape. Then, you can see immediately when a tool is missing from its place.

Gymea lilies

The fantastic prehistoric-looking Gymea lilies (*Doryanthes excelsa*), from a genus of just two species, are flowering now. Their huge red heads, held on javelins up to 6 metres tall, look spectacular against a clear, blue sky. The inflorescences are, in fact, dozens of small flowers held together like a glowing torch: the single head, in velvety burgundy, cerise and red, emerges from a rosette—up to 3 metres wide—of sword-like leaves. Native to the east coast of Australia, the lily thrives on the Hawkesbury sandstone of the Sydney Basin, and is one of the largest lilies in the world.

The glorious Gymea lily, in the shadow of Sydney's Centrepoint Tower

5 June

World Environment Day

World Environment Day takes place on 5 June each year. The organisers encourage people around the world to conserve water and energy and to reduce their carbon footprint. Minimising the use of plastic bags, drinking tap, rather than bottled, water and turning off lights and power points are all part of a worldwide movement towards protecting the planet.

Gardeners can contribute to the effort. Good garden-keeping includes practising heavy mulching, which assists in reducing water use and the need for chemical weed killers and pesticides. Except in areas where bushfire concerns are a first consideration, trees can protect roofs from heat (obviating the excessive use of air-conditioners) and consume carbon dioxide. Growing our own vegetables avoids carbon emissions created by transporting food from distant markets. With the continued improvement in organic pest-control methods and horticultural oils to combat garden diseases, we no longer need to use chemicals in the garden, protecting our health along with that of the birds and the bees—and the environment.

6 June

Drawing the garden

Drawing up your garden—or even part of it—on paper before you start digging will crystallise what is possible and avoid expensive mistakes. And winter is the perfect time to contemplate what you can create, and to try your hand at garden design. After measuring up the garden, take a scale rule, pencil, paper and rubber: draw the outline of the garden, and then mark in the garden beds. You can even create to-scale cut-outs of trees and key structural elements and move them around on your master plan, or overlays of tracing, or butter, paper, to follow the habit of Humphry Repton, the eighteenth-century landscape designer, who presented to clients a book—known as a 'Red Book'—that illustrated scenes before and after his proposed improvements, to demonstrate the merits of his ideas.

Beautiful trees

A beautiful tree can be just as special as a unique piece of sculpture. Two of my favourite trees are a magnificent horse chestnut (*Aesculus hippocastanum*) at Newby Hall, in the north of England, and an ancient English oak (*Quercus robur*) that has fallen onto its side, but is still thriving, at Bentley, in Tasmania. They are living works of art.

The glorious horse chestnut at Newby Hall, in the north of England

Tuberoses

It's time to plant summer-flowering bulbs, among them the gloriously scented tuberoses (*Polianthes tuberosa*), greatly loved for bridal bouquets. Lilium bulbs will be on sale in nurseries; plant them now to enjoy their scented trumpet flowers in early summer. They enjoy having their feet in the shade and heads in the sun. *Lilium regale* and *L. longiflorum* will provide elegant stands of white flowers by Christmas Day, while the heavenly *L. auratum* will fill the garden with scent and colour in January. The yellow pollen from any of these lilies will stain garments if you brush past the stamens, so cut the stamens off as the flower buds open. If you do get the pollen on fabric, do not rub it; remove it quickly with sticky tape.

Don't forget to plant a brick with your lily of the valley (*Convallaria majalis*), which will bloom in October: it loves being close to generated heat, and so makes a perfect edging plant along a brick wall, such as at Nooroo, at Mount Wilson in the Blue Mountains.

For a display of lily of the valley like this (at Nooroo, Mount Wilson) you will need to provide the warmth of a brick!

9 June

Fernando Caruncho

Fernando Caruncho (b. 1957), who designs public and private gardens in his native Spain, as well as throughout Europe, the Far East and the United States, is known for the symmetry and geometric style of his work. In *Mirrors of Paradise: The Gardens of Fernando Caruncho*, he notes that nature does not design in straight lines, but man, in garden design, uses geometry to express his art. 'Any good garden or landscape can be inspired by geometry, even if its true lines are concealed by the irregular outlines of organic shapes. The straight line reminds us of the presence of man, while the curve represents a return to idyllic nature.' This is good news for those who hanker after formality in their garden.

10 June

Selecting trees

Winter is the time to purchase the deciduous trees that you might have selected during open garden visits in autumn, choosing those with spectacular leaf colouring. Whether intended as a specimen in a lawn, to provide summer shade, as a small tree to add scale to a courtyard garden, or to emphasise the entrance to your property, many trees are best purchased bare-rooted, in winter. This is the most economical way to buy trees, often from mail-order growers; the shock of replanting is reduced when the tree is dormant and the desired shape is best created when branches are bare.

11 June

Here is the recipe for my favourite comfort food: risotto.

Risotto

3 leeks, washed, peeled and finely sliced
   (white sections only)
1 onion, finely chopped
several cloves garlic, crushed and chopped
2 tablespoons olive oil
60 g butter
2 cups Arborio rice
1.5–2 litres hot stock (chicken and/or lamb)
salt and cracked pepper
50 g Reggiano parmesan cheese, shaved

Fry leeks with onion and garlic in olive oil and 30 g butter, until clear, but not browned. Remove from pan and set aside. In the same pan, sauté rice until clear. Return onion mix to pan, and slowly add stock, ¼ cup at a time. Don't add too much at once: the rice should be 'crying out' for the stock. Stir constantly and continue to add stock until all is absorbed, or until rice is al dente. Turn off heat, stir in remaining butter, and season with salt and pepper. Serve with shaved parmesan. (I also like to serve with cubes of baked sweet potato or steamed fresh peas.) Serves six.

Villa d'Este

There are fountains, and there are fountains. And then there is the Villa d'Este. Designed by Pirro Ligorio in 1550, and set in the hills to the east of Rome, Villa d'Este is a prime example of the spectacular engineering employed to create the water features central to Italy's High Renaissance period. The Terrace of One Hundred Fountains runs the breadth of the garden, supporting cascades and fountains in almost every style imaginable. At the base of the garden, the extraordinary Water Organ Fountain erupts into water jets and wide waterfalls every thirty minutes: it must surely be at the pinnacle of garden art.

The pinnacle of the art—the Water Organ Fountain at the Villa d'Este at Tivoli, close to Rome

Winter bulbs

Even if you live in a warm climate, you will probably enjoy some winter-flowering bulbs in your garden, just to mark the change in the season. The snowflake (*Leucojum* spp.), a genus of ten species, is among the easiest of the winter bulbs to cultivate and will mass out happily in all climates except in the tropics. The delicate bulb is native to North Africa and the southern Mediterranean, and bears white, bell-shaped pendant flowers.

Snowdrops (*Galanthus nivalis*) require a cooler climate and are a little trickier to grow well. Among the coveted varieties are the large-flowered *G. elwesii* 'Comet'. Divide them every three or four years to ensure continued flowering; don't allow them to become too crowded, particularly among more strongly growing bulbs, as this will restrict flowering.

The coveted *Galanthus elwesii* requires a cool climate.

Allerton Gardens

While it is mid-winter south of the equator, in the Northern Hemisphere it is summer, and the temperature in many countries can soar above 40 degrees Celsius. In Hawaii, dark, cool shade is created by the indigenous coconut palm. At Allerton Gardens, on the island of Kauai, the palms bend luxuriantly over the river; as young trees they were weighed down with rocks by Hideo Teshima, the head gardener for fifty-six years.

Bromeliads also flourish at Allerton Gardens, on the Hawaiian island of Kauai.

Evergreens

Every gardener, I would suggest, needs a selection of evergreen species in their repertoire. Pruned into charming specimen trees, or trimmed to a dense hedge, evergreens can form the backbone of a garden, and provide shelter from winds that can hit at any time of year, particularly on coastal sites.

Apart from some of the well-known names, which include lilly pillies, murrayas and camellias, there are plenty of beautiful evergreens to choose from. The *Calliandra*, a genus of some 200 species of evergreen shrubs and trees, bears flowers in red, pink or cream, and is an excellent choice for exposed sites. With crimson flowers in late winter and spring, the *Metrosideros excelsa* (often called the powder puff tree) looks superb when pruned and combined with the white flowers of the tough-leaved evergreen Indian hawthorn (*Rhaphiolepis indica*), and its leathery leaves will happily withstand the onslaught of salt winds. Add to the mix the frost-hardy escallonia, another valuable plant for a coastal site.

Evergreen trees add structure to a large garden or park.

More choice is provided by the tough *Coprosma repens*, native to New Zealand and flowering orange in counterpoint to the grey-leaved coastal rosemary (*Westringia fruticosa*), with its lilac flowers. One of the best plants for frontline defence against salt winds is the oleander (*Nerium oleander*), which will also tolerate a hot, western position and little water. Among the cultivars are 'Mrs Fred Roeding', which grows to about a metre, and 'Petite Pink' and 'Petite Salmon', lower growing varieties.

16 June

Looking over fences!

Early morning walks, when travelling, can be a great source of ideas. Not long ago, during such an amble around an inner Melbourne suburb, I peered over the front fence of an Edwardian house. A gently winding path of dark bricks arranged in a herringbone led to the black-painted front door. To one side, a wide border housed a ribbon of several of the American redbud tree (*Cercis canadensis* 'Forest Pansy'). This deciduous cultivar, related to the taller growing Judas tree (*C. siliquastrum*) from southern Europe, the Middle East and China, can grow to some 6 metres and bears cerise, fringed flowers, on bare wood, just before the burgundy-coloured heart-shaped leaves emerge. (In autumn the foliage takes on stunning colours before leaf fall.) Below, a rib of deep-purple to black tulips flowered; perhaps they were 'Queen of the Night', 'Negrita' or 'Blue Champion'. In front of them was an edge of the pewter-leaved hellebore (*Helleborus* × *ballardiae*), which demands full sun in cool-climate gardens, but in warmer areas grows well in shade, particularly in a southerly position. (If you garden in more humid climates, you will have better success with *H.* × *sternii* 'Boughton Beauty', with its blue-green jagged-toothed leaves.) Gorgeous!

17 June

The lace-cape flowers of *Viburnum macrocephalum* f. *keteleeri*

Viburnums

While many of the viburnums are coveted for their luscious scent in spring, through winter their wonderful berries—in a range of colours from yellow and orange to red and burgundy—make them a must-have for the cool-climate garden. Not only do they add interest and cheer to the season; they also provide an endless supply of 'garden pick' for flower arrangements for the house.

At Dumbarton Oaks, in Washington—one of Beatrix Farrand's greatest designs

19 June

Beatrix Farrand

Beatrix Jones Farrand, the American garden designer, was born in New York City on this day in 1872. The pre-eminent designer of the so-called golden age of American gardens, Farrand worked mainly on the east coast of the United States, where the privileged from Boston and New York spent their summers, and in the rarefied mountain areas to the west of those cities.

Farrand was influenced by the work of the English designer Gertrude Jekyll, whom she visited early in her career. Later, Farrand rescued Jekyll's garden plans from a charity sale, eventually bequeathing them to the University of California, Berkeley Campus, where they remain today. Like Jekyll, Farrand employed the structure and scale of Italian Renaissance gardens to great effect, using water, stone and evergreen plants, along with the soft blues and greys of Mediterranean species.

Perhaps Farrand's greatest legacy is Dumbarton Oaks, the wonderful garden in Washington, DC, created over some forty years, in collaboration with her client, Mildred Bliss. It is something of a secret, however, that she also laid out an important landscape in England: a 15-hectare garden around Dartington Hall, in Devon. In 1933, Farrand wrote to the hall's owners: 'If you like Dumbarton Oaks, let us work to make Dartington its English Fellow. Dartington is starting with infinitely more beauty'.

Dartington Hall, Beatrix Farrand's only commission in the United Kingdom

Much of the garden at Dartington spans a valley, at the base of which a green theatre, in the tradition of gardens such as Villa Reale, in Tuscany, was created. Opening up overgrown woodland walks of yew and holly, Farrand added layered underplantings with collections of rhododendrons, camellias and magnolias. She included an azalea dell, and herbaceous borders in shades of cream, blue and purple. Farrand also created a much-admired quadrangle garden. Among the major works of art exhibited throughout the grounds is Henry Moore's sculpture *Reclining Figure*, reached through an avenue of ancient chestnuts.

The English garden designer Percy Cane worked on Dartington from 1945, when Farrand felt she was no longer able to travel to England, although she remained in regular correspondence with the owners, her last letter written in February 1959, six months before her death. Cane applauded Farrand's work, noting, during a presentation to the Royal Horticultural Society, in 1954, 'When I first saw Dartington Hall, I wondered if its gardens could be made more beautiful than they already were … the walks … were made just where they fitted most easily into the rising slopes, and needed only to be left as they were'.

20 June

Dry-stone walls

A wonderful dry-stone wall—which John Hawkins has dubbed 'The Great Wall of Chudleigh'—surrounds the home paddock at Bentley, in the north of Tasmania.

The wall contains dolerite stones of slightly different colours, as they were collected from different paddocks throughout the Chudleigh Valley. A hole in the bottom of a dry-stone wall, which allows for drainage, is known as a smoot.

'The Great Wall of Chudleigh'

21 June

The winter solstice

It's a tradition: plant cloves of garlic on this, the shortest day of the year, the winter solstice. (And harvest your garlic on the longest day, after the foliage has died back.) Home-grown garlic is milder than that bought from commercial nurserymen, and the cheap, imported garlic you find in supermarkets has been bleached, and then doused in various pesticides and herbicides. In addition, as with all imported produce, under Australian quarantine law, imported garlic is treated with methyl bromide. This fumigant is used to control a number of pests, but is also a fire extinguishing agent, a solvent and a refrigerant: it is listed as toxic to humans and animals! Garlic is easy to grow: simply push a clove—pointed end up—into the soil. Use a soluble fertiliser though spring and summer. Like most vegies, garlic loves the sun.

22 June

Avocados

My Italian neighbour has lived in her house for the fifty-eight years of her married life. Each morning, as I walk my dog, I peer over her back fence to see how her orchard and vegetable garden are progressing. She is the epitome of a good gardener, with her tomatoes perfectly dusted and staked, her onions and garlic in neat rows, her broccoli flourishing through winter, her avocado trees (*Persea americana*) carefully pruned to encourage optimum fruit production. Native to Central America and the West Indies, this medium-size tree will be perfectly happy in cooler climates if provided with frost protection when young. If you live south of the warm temperate zones, seek out varieties like 'Zutano', 'Fuerte' and 'Bacon'. You need two trees to ensure good cropping. Fruit is picked when still firm, to ripen indoors.

23 June

Borrowed views

The idea of *shakkei* (borrowed scenery) is central to the Japanese landscape design aesthetic. Probably practised, even unwittingly, in most gardening cultures, *shakkei*—the inclusion of a neighbour's trees at the edges of a garden, or distant mountains to which the eye is drawn—will make any garden appear larger than it is. This principle is crucial to the relationship between a garden and its environment. And winter, when many plants in the garden are bare, is the perfect time to assess such design elements.

Shakkei is displayed perfectly at Murin-an, on the east side of Kyoto. Through the judicious pruning of the pines and maples in the garden, the surrounding hills can be appreciated from the quiet of the tea house. Murin-an was created in 1896, by Aritomo Yamagata, a politician during the Meiji period, and is an excellent example of private gardens of the time. Less highly stylised than earlier Japanese gardens, it seeks to create a naturalistic landscape.

The design aesthetic of borrowed views is perfectly displayed at Murin-an, Kyoto

24 June

Dianthus

The gloriously scented dianthus 'Mrs Sinkins' grows best in cool to cold climates, although you will see her for sale in nurseries in humid parts of the country. With silver-grey, spiky foliage, she blooms for months, given the right conditions, with white semi-double flowers that have a rich, clove-like scent. She was bred by the English nurseryman John Thomas Sinkins and named for his wife, Catherine. This lovely, extremely fragrant dianthus first went on sale in 1872.

25 June

This Imperial garden was influenced, it is said, by Murasaki Shikibu's *The Tale of Genji*.

The Tale of Genji

One of the world's first novels, *Genji monogatari* (*The Tale of Genji*), was written in around 1008 by Murasaki Shikibu, a noblewoman of the Japanese court, during the Heian period (781–1185). The 54-chapter novel is considered a literary masterpiece and an important historical document. It is thought that, with its descriptions of idyllic gardens and its reflection upon the fleeting beauty embodied by nature, the book was a major influence on the design of the great stroll garden Katsura Rikyu, in the western part of Kyoto. The garden is a sublime example of the ideal of *kirei sabi* (refined beauty) through rustic simplicity. Created from about 1610, by Prince Toshihito, the property became a haven for artists, writers and garden lovers. Katsura

Rikyu was completed by Toshihito's son, the scholarly Prince Toshitada, and was designed to lead guests on a journey: Toshitada hosted tea ceremonies, moon-viewing and boating parties when the reflections of buildings, and of trees, could be best appreciated.

26 June

Cheesecake

Isn't nature marvellous? In the coldest months of the year, when you crave oranges and lemons, the citrus trees are laden with juicy fruit rich in vitamin C. Friends may be offering bags of lemons—and the best way to start the day is surely with a whole lemon squeezed into a cup of boiling water. And, just to counteract such a healthy start, here is a recipe, given to me by a friend, for the most delicious cheesecake you will encounter. A little is good for you. Truly.

Lemon and almond ricotta cheesecake

250 g blanched almonds
65 g plain flour, or, for a gluten-free option, ground almonds
zest 6 lemons, finely grated
225 g unsalted butter
250 g caster sugar
6 eggs, separated
400 g ricotta
juice 3 lemons
½ teaspoon vanilla essence (optional)

Preheat oven to 150°C. Grease a cake tin of 24 centimetres diameter, with removable base, and line with greaseproof paper. Chop almonds finely in a food processor, leaving some a little coarser, for texture. Combine with flour or almond meal and lemon zest. In a separate bowl, cream together butter and sugar, stir in egg yolks one at a time, then add almond mixture. In a separate bowl, lightly beat ricotta with vanilla essence. Add lemon juice. In another bowl, beat egg whites to form stiff peaks. Fold into the almond mixture and add ricotta. Spoon mixture into tin and bake for around 40 minutes, or until almost set: a skewer inserted into the middle should come out clean. Remove from tin while still warm. Serve with strawberries or blueberries, and vanilla ice cream or clotted cream.

27 June

Hellebores

Cut away the scrappy leaves of the hellebores so that the delicate flowers are easy to see when they start to emerge. In cold climates, the white flowers of *Helleborus niger* appear like splotches of fallen snow on brilliantly coloured leaves if planted beneath a tree that takes on rich colours each autumn. And, a little later in the season, the glamorous black-flowering hellebore (*H. × hybridus* 'Plum Purple') looks wonderful emerging through a carpet of fallen pink magnolia petals.

28 June

Albert Namatjira

Born on this day in 1902 into the Arunta tribe at Hermannsburg, in the Northern Territory, Albert Namatjira was the first Aboriginal Australian painter to achieve wide acclaim. His first one-man exhibition, of forty landscape paintings, in Melbourne in 1938, was a sell-out. It is possible to experience the landscape that inspired him by walking the Larapinta Trail—200 kilometres through the West MacDonnell Ranges, in Central Australia—where the ghost gums that Namatjira loved still create an awe-inspiring sense of place.

29 June

More vegies

It's mid-winter, but there is still time to plant a second crop of cool-weather vegies, and more of those that are happy in most months of the year. Sow more carrots, leeks, broccoli and beetroot, along with broadbeans. Keep up the soluble fertiliser and watch for thrip on your Brussels sprouts: spray with Yates Success or Eco-oil.

The fabulous colours of the red bud mallee

The red bud mallee

The fascinating red bud mallee (*Eucalyptus pachyphylla*) is native to Central Australia but is popular as a street tree in many of Perth's suburbs. It bears glorious acid-yellow blossom from late winter to summer. The blossom bursts from large-ribbed buds which turn a deep pink before they split to reveal a mass of perfectly arranged butter-yellow stamens. Like most of the mallees, it is a drought-tolerant species, and grows to some 6 metres with a single or multiple trunks decorated with peeling gray bark.

Another member of the genus *Eucalyptus*, the beautiful weeping 'Silver Princess' (*E. caesia*), is native to the wheat belt of West Australia. This mallee has silvery, powdery stems and gorgeous gumnuts; it is greatly loved by honeyeaters and parrots. Like many Australian native plants, however, the 'Silver Princess' resents summer humidity.

July

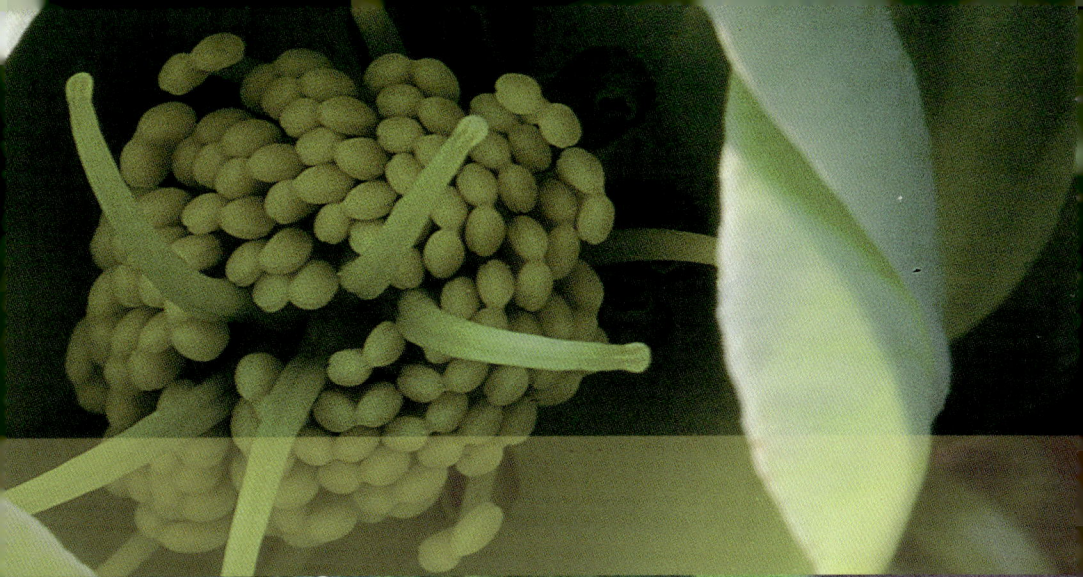

1 July

Rose girls

The English aviator Amy Johnson, after whom the horticulturalist Alister Clark named a beautiful rose, was born on this day in 1903. In May 1930, Johnson arrived at Eagle Farm Airport in Brisbane in her de Havilland Moth, after a nineteen-day solo flight from England. The gorgeous, fragrant, very vigorous rose that bears her name is an apricot-pink repeat-flowering climber, and was bred by Clark in 1931.

The rose 'Amy Johnson'

2 July

Hatfield

Elizabeth Tudor, second daughter of Henry VII, was born on this day in 1492. Her namesake, Queen Elizabeth I, spent much of her childhood in the grounds of Hatfield House, home of the Salisburys and one of the most applauded gardens in England, largely reconstructed, over the past half-century, by Mollie, Dowager Marchioness of Salisbury. It was at Hatfield, under a spreading oak that continues to thrive today, that Elizabeth was told that her half-sister, Mary, had died, and that she had become Queen Elizabeth I.

The long vista at Hatfield House

3 July

Celia Thaxter

It is interesting to reflect upon the meaning of gardens, the repositories of so much information—and not just on the plants. Gardens convey messages of gender, class, influence and success, of economics and demographics. Most of us would agree that gardens provide a site for creativity. For some, in particular women, I would suggest, the creation of a garden also gives comfort and solace, sometimes after the loss of family or familiar surroundings. You might imagine that such a need contributed, at least in part, to the creation of Celia Thaxter's garden on Appledore Island, the largest among the Isles of Shoals, some 15 kilometres off the coast from the charming New Hampshire fishing town of Portsmouth, in the United States.

'The very act of planting a seed in the earth has in it to me something beautiful. I always do it with a joy that is largely mixed with awe', Celia wrote in her book *An Island Garden*, published in 1894. 'I watch my garden beds as they are sown, and think how one of God's exquisite miracles is going on beneath the dark earth out of sight.'

Celia was born in Portsmouth in 1835. When she was twelve, her father, after eight years as lighthouse keeper on nearby White Island, built a luxury resort hotel on Appledore. It became a gathering place for the literary and artistic personalities of the east coast of America during the latter part of the nineteenth century, with Harriet Beecher Stowe and Samuel Longfellow among the guests. Celia was sixteen years old when she married Levi Thaxter, her father's business partner and her tutor. Ill health forced Levi to return to the mainland; he took their three sons with him while Celia remained on Appledore. The creation of her garden over the next few decades was perhaps Celia's way of surviving the loss of her family.

Spring colour ...

She built her flower garden, which she called 'the great laboratory of nature', a few hundred metres from the wild, rocky shore of this 40-hectare granite island. The flowers in the garden were for picking: the snowdrops, lilies, cornflowers, poppies, hollyhocks and delphiniums that grew in nine rectangular beds filled the hotel, arranged in bottles and glass vases. 'The first small bed', she wrote, 'contained only Marigolds, fire-coloured blossoms which were the joy of my heart and the delight of my eyes'.

Such detail was used to reconstruct an exact replica of Celia's garden in its original position, when the Shoals Marine Laboratory, the University of Cornell, several mainland garden clubs and their volunteers joined forces in 1977. The garden is laid out in a rectangle, 17 metres long and 4 metres wide. Beds that run the length and breadth of the boundary house species roses, and a wide variety of perennial and annual flowering plants. The garden is open to visitors on Wednesdays during July and August.

4 July

Independence Day

Independence Day in the United States celebrates the liberation of the American colonies from Great Britain, one of the factors that led to the European settlement of Australia. George Washington, the first president of United States, from 1789 to 1797, owned several vast estates along the Potomac River, in Virginia, including River Farm, which now serves as the headquarters of the American Horticultural Society. Among many hero trees that remain in the garden today is the state tree of Virginia: the glorious flowering dogwood (*Cornus florida*).

5 July

Bend winter prunings to create great edges for garden beds.

Use those prunings

Do you know anyone who owns a vineyard? If so, beg them for the grapevine prunings. While they are still supple, wind them into wreaths which you can use as table decorations, or as Christmas wreaths. Or, weave them into hurdles to create smart edgings which will add a country aesthetic to your vegie garden. If you don't have access to vineyard prunings, willow, hazelnut and some fruit trees can be coppiced to encourage tall, straight, whippy rods, which can then be cut and, when half dry, woven and bound into baskets, fences and hurdles.

6 July

At the first hint of warm winter weather the Banksian roses burst into bloom.

Banksian roses

In warm temperate climates the Banksian roses are already flowering. Of the four forms of the *Rosa banksiae* in cultivation today, the wild-flowering *R. banksiae normalis* is the most vigorous, reaching some 9 metres in warm climates. The white-flowering, almost thornless *R. banksiae banksiae* and the well-known *R. banksiae lutea*, with bright-yellow double flowers, are more popular with gardeners. *R. banksiae lutescens*, introduced to the horticultural world in 1870, is slightly less vigorous than the other forms; it also blooms yellow and is very fragrant.

Serendipity

Serendipity plays a part in great garden-making, as it does in life, I suppose. In my warm temperate garden, a *Magnolia × soulangiana* is in bloom: generous goblets of pink are splashed with cerise. Underneath, the deep-purple blooms of a wide ribbon of *Helleborus × hybridus* 'Purpureus' team perfectly with the magnolia flowers, and the backdrop of the hen and chicken fern (*Asplenium bulbiferum*). Native throughout much of Australia and New Zealand, this is a gentle-looking fern, similar to the maidenhair fern (*Adiantum aethiopicum*), with stunning purple-black stems. I couldn't have planned a better effect—but it was just chance. Serendipity. For added drama, I may one day add cerise or black tulips to this arrangement.

Big rewards for little effort—the gloriously scented *Coelogyne* Unchained Melody

Coelogynes

If you have orchids in your garden you will have noticed that the cymbidiums and phalaeonopsis are putting on an extraordinary performance, as long as they receive a few hours of morning sun each day. And suddenly, after a year of neglect, half-a-dozen yellow-and-white sprays of the lovely coelo-gynes, many native to the Malay highlands, are filling the whole house with their heady fragrance. Among the easiest to grow is the stunning *Coelogyne* Unchained Melody. Like all orchids, it loves a crowd, so allow it to fill, and spill out of, its pot. Don't cut off the spent spikes of your cymbidium orchids; simply trim the dead flowers, as new spires of flowers can form.

The usual rules of botanical nomenclature (see also 23 May) do not always apply to the naming of orchids. Orchids are the only group of plants where hybrid names, known as grex epithets, are registered with the Royal Horticultural Society in London. None of the hybrids, whether human-made or naturally occurring, is given inverted commas. For instance, the hybrid between the two *Coelogyne* species *cristata* and *flaccida* is always called *Coelogyne* Unchained Melody.

9 July

Citrus leaf gall

Examine your citrus for citrus leaf gall—unsightly lumps and bumps in leaves, and, in serious infestations, on stems—a sure sign that the citrus gall wasp has laid eggs on your plants. This is a serious pest which, if left, will quickly kill your trees and spread through your neighbourhood. Cutting back the infected areas is the only remedy. Dispose of the diseased cuttings in tied bags, in the garbage—or burn them. If left until mid August, when the weather may start to warm, the eggs will hatch and larvae emerge, making further control impossible.

10 July

Daphne

My daphne has burst into bloom. Said to be a pernickety plant, daphne will happily flower each July, even in a warm temperate climate, if given a south-erly or easterly position. It can, indeed, suddenly turn up its toes—but that is a price you may be willing to pay for its heavenly scent, which will fill your house, even from just a few sprigs. Add a wide edge of the blue-flowering grape hyacinths (*Muscari armeniacum*): they look marvellous together in a shallow bowl. As daphne is not difficult to propagate, take cuttings from sections that do not bloom this season.

Over the past week or so, the wisteria has been limbering up for spring drama: fat buds have appeared on spurs that were pruned last summer. Although winter is the time to wield the secateurs for many species, don't be tempted to prune wisteria now, unless flowers are forming where they are not wanted. Most problems with wisteria not blooming can be explained by mid winter pruning.

11 July

In the foyer of the Shangri La Hotel, Singapore, the delicate *Phalaeonopsis* butterfly orchid

12 July

Beautiful bark

It's mid winter; have you stroked your trees yet? Once the scarlet and purple foliage of the oaks and maples and the shimmering golds and butter yellows of the birch and tulip trees are gone, and can no longer distract and delight us,

The beauty of bark: clockwise from top left, *Casuarina* spp., *Pinus radiata*, *Melaleuca quinquinervia*, *Banksia marginata*

the colours, textures and idiosyncrasies of their barks are revealed. Along with myrtles and crepe myrtles, birch and several rhododendrons, many trees are prized for their bark, which can take on special hues in warm winter light.

The peeling, cinnamon-coloured bark of the paperbark maple (*Acer griseum*), discovered in China in 1901 by the plant hunter Ernest Wilson, ensures it a place in many gardens. The late-colouring Japanese maple *Acer palmatum* 'Sango kaku' (also known as 'Senkaki') is a lovely small tree with coral bark that intensifies in colour with winter. The bark is almost fluorescent on young wood, tempting some gardeners to coppice it as a hedge. Many of the camellias have fascinating bark: *Camellia yunnanensis*, from southern China, features gorgeous red bark (which you can almost rub off) along with its fragile white single blooms. Related to the camellia, and native to China, *Stewartia sinensis* has beautiful red bark that peels in autumn to reveal a smooth grey trunk. The cinnamon bark myrtle (*Luma apiculata*) grows to a medium-size tree, with the bonus of flaking, cinnamon-coloured bark and aromatic leaves.

The snow gum (*Eucalyptus pauciflora* subsp. *niphophila*), native to the high country of the Snowy Mountains, takes on greens and browns, caramels, russets and reds in winter, in the low, golden light of late afternoon. The fragile, milky light of the winter dawn illuminates the cream honey-filled blossoms that cover the giant paperbarks (*Melaleuca quinquenervia*), at home in the Lachlan Swamps in Sydney's Centennial Park. At this time of the year, their peeling bark takes on a range of russet colours, from ochre and caramel to taupe and cream. Plane trees, liquidambars, gordonias and Chinese elms, as well as some of the deciduous conifers, also have lovely bark.

13 July

Grevilleas

The grevilleas will have suddenly burst into multicoloured flowers, including the hybrid *Grevillea* 'Robyn Gordon', which, in frost-free areas, is covered in cream, brush-like blooms held amid fine, teal-green foliage at this time of the year. Other stunning hybrids and varieties include 'Sandra Gordon', 'Ned Kelly', 'Superb' and the luscious 'Coconut Ice'. An added bonus is that grevilleas, along with their cousins in the Proteaceae family, play host to those brilliantly coloured rainbow lorikeets, who feast on the nectar in a noisy, joyful chorus. But take care if you are an asthma sufferer, as some grevillea cultivars can aggravate symptoms.

14 July

Banksias

I love those big bad banksia men—the inflorescences of saw banksia (*Banksia serrata*)—but they terrified me as a child. The fat, green to yellow candle-like blooms of this species are held during July and August among last year's flowers, which have turned into the rather frightening seed pods that inspired the famous Australian children's author May Gibbs to write *The Complete Adventures of Snugglepot and Cuddlepie*. Umber candles glow on the heath banksia (*B. ericifolia*), which is native to the sandstone areas of New South Wales. And gorgeous red flowers are held erect on the stiff branches of the scarlet banksia (*B. coccinea*), native to Western Australia. In the same

Proteaceae family, the Tasmanian waratah 'Shady Lady' (*Telopea truncata*) is yellow-blooming, fast-growing and frost-hardy, but, like most native plants, demands good drainage.

Banksia baxteri

15 July

Rhubarb

Mid winter is the time to plant rhubarb crowns, so that they will grow well during the warm months. A perennial vegetable, rhubarb is productive for several years, so it appreciates its own dedicated bed. Provide plenty of moisture and fertiliser and a sunny spot to encourage well-coloured, sweet stems. Harvest the outside stems, which are high in vitamin C, in summer, but discard the leaves, which, high in oxalic acid, are toxic. Divide plants after about five years.

Citrus

Have you harvested your citrus yet? If so, it's time to fertilise. If not, keep watering! And prevent thick skins on the fruit by spraying with a solution of magnesium and zinc.

The genus *Citrus*, which contains about fifteen species, is part of the Rutaceae family. Although originally from South-East Asia and New Caledonia, citrus have been cultivated in Europe since pre-history: they are pruned to provide shady avenues, or espaliered to form scented allées, in gardens around the Mediterranean. They are happy growing in Versailles-style wooden tubs, or in terracotta. In most parts of Australia you won't need a *limonaria*—a heated glasshouse, often elaborately designed, popular in European gardens—to grow citrus. Nor will you need the solid-silver receptacles favoured by Louis XIV at Versailles!

When we think of citrus, we think first, perhaps, of oranges and lemons. The orange (*C. sinensis*), with its glossy, green leaves and white, scented, waxy blossom, reaches up to 8 metres. Lemons (*C. limon*) come mainly in three varieties. The less acidic 'Meyer' is thought to be a cross between an orange and a lemon; it tolerates cold and frost, and bears fruit with smooth, thin skin. 'Eureka', almost thornless, and bearing fruit from spring through to autumn, is usually chosen for warmer climates. 'Lisbon' is a thorny variety bearing large, juicy fruit. Also popular is 'Lots 'a Lemons', a dwarf form of the 'Meyer', which will reach about 1.5 metres.

However, the *Citrus* genus includes many more species than these. There is the Tahitian lime (*C. aurantifolia*), for example, which bears heavily scented flowers that are followed by delicious fruit, ideal for use in cooking and drinks. If you wait until the fruit turns yellow before picking, the flavour will be richer. Mandarins (*C. reticulata*) are many people's favourite fruit; the very juicy tangelo (*C. × tangelo* 'Minneola'), a hybrid created from a mandarin and a grapefruit, is the easiest to peel. Cumquats, either the elliptical *Fortunella margarita* 'Nagami', or the round *F. japonica* 'Marumi', are somewhat bitter, best suited for marmalade-making; the egg-shaped 'Meiwa' cumquat (*F. crassifolia*) is sweet, however.

Following pages: The historic garden is again looking wonderful at Otahuna Lodge, a luxury country house hotel near Christchurch on New Zealand's South Island.

17 July

Frensham

'It is not the gardeners who count, but God who makes it grow. We are God's fellow-workers, and you are God's garden.' Winifred West, the founder and headmistress of Frensham, a girls school at Mittagong in New South Wales, quoted from 1 Corinthians 3:6–9 in her address to the school community of students, teachers and parents on this day in 1963. West regarded the garden she created at the school as an integral part of the education of young women, the canvas upon which her philosophies of shared information and service to others might be drawn. For West the garden was a metaphor for living, demonstrating that the presence of beauty was essential through every aspect of life.

18 July

The smooth-barked angophoras

Among the loveliest of Australian trees, and closely related to the eucalypts, angophoras can often be found clinging to the sandstone cliffs around Sydney Harbour. The smooth-barked apple (*Angophora costata*), with its twisted

The smooth, pink-trunked angophora clings to sandstone cliffs around Sydney Harbour

branches that often play host to clouds of sulphur-crested cockatoos, must have been an extraordinary sight for the first European settlers as they sailed through the Heads, into the harbour.

19 July

Winter pruning

There is plenty to prune in the garden at this time of the year. Among the main reasons for pruning any plant is the promotion of correct growth; many deciduous trees can be pruned now, therefore, while their branches are bare and you can ascertain the shape you wish to create. Pruning can also promote abundant flowering, so the decision about when, and how, to prune depends upon when a plant bears flowers, and sets fruit: on this season's or last season's growth. In short, don't prune when or where flower buds are forming.

Pears and apples set fruit on two- to three-year-old wood, while most stone-fruit trees bear on the previous season's wood. If you garden in the average city space, however, you may want to prune these trees hard to restrict fruit production—unless you have plenty of friends and neighbours with whom you can share. An open vase shape is easy to maintain, especially if you prune the tree to a serviceable height.

It's time to prune hydrangeas; cut back—to two sets of fat buds—those stems that flowered earlier in the year. The plants will flower, in mid-summer, on the stems that did not flower in the previous season. Don't waste the cuttings: plant sections 10 centimetres long, with two sets of buds attached, into propagating mix, and position them where they will catch the winter sun. If they aren't allowed to dry out, hydrangeas are among the easiest of all plants to propagate. And they make great loose, informal hedges, or, planted en masse, stunning borders, flowering in December.

20 July

Charles Sturt

Captain Charles Sturt entered the Simpson Desert on this day in 1845, during his search for an inland sea, and discovered there the desert pea (*Swainsona formosa*) near a watercourse that he named Cooper Creek. A member of the

Fabaceae family, this red-flowering, ground-hugging creeper is endemic to the drier regions of Australia and was mentioned several times by Sturt in his journal *Narrative of an Expedition into Central Australia*, an account of his expedition. Sturt's desert pea was named the floral emblem of South Australia in 1961.

21 July

Beautiful and useful

I have long been an advocate of the philosophy that anything we have should be both beautiful and useful. Scent plays a big part in that little homily: it is so evocative of the different times in our lives, so important to each day. A fragrance can bring to mind a certain person; a smell of a particular suntan oil can evoke memories of a summer past.

It's impossible to nominate the flower with the most beautiful scent. Gardenias bring to mind a beautifully set table at Christmas, while the Bourbon rose 'Madame Isaac Pereire' produces, surely, the richest rose scent. The fragrance of *Viburnum carlesii* always takes me back to Sissinghurst, where I first encountered it, and the delicate scents of magnolia and wisteria fill me with excitement, as they promise that spring has arrived.

22 July

Strawberries

It's time to plant strawberries. They are easy to grow well, and will fruit from early summer through to autumn. They are happy in pots, or can be popped into any spaces available in a cottage garden layout, or employed as edging plants; you can even cram them into spaces in a dry-stone wall. Plant them in full sun, about 40 centimetres apart in garden beds. Mix in a complete fertiliser to the soil before planting, and apply potassium-rich fertiliser to encourage flower and fruit set. Make sure the fruit does not rest on the soil. Among the varieties available are 'Strawberry Supreme', a conical-shaped, disease-resistant cultivar that combines the advantages of sweet, firm fruit with a high vitamin C content and a long cropping season; 'Bravo' (often called 'Supreme'), a full-flavoured, sweet variety; the aromatic 'Toyonoka'; and the full-flavoured and early fruiting 'Chandler', good for jam-making.

Copied the world over, the white garden at Sissinghurst

23 July

Sissinghurst

The White Garden at Sissinghurst, in the English county of Kent, is at its peak in July, when its centrepiece, the climbing *Rosa mulliganii*, covering an arbour, is in full flower. The regal lilies (*Lilium regale*) are rising tall from their tight corsets of clipped box; the *Crambe cordifolia* is flowering in clouds of fine, white blossom, along with white poppies, verbenas and geraniums. The soft greys of dusty miller (*Senecio cineraria*) and lamb's ear (*Stachys lanata*), and of silver-leaved tobacco (*Nicotiana* spp.) and sea hollies (*Eryngium* spp.) tie the scheme together. If you can visit, go late in the afternoon, when the light is golden and the crowds have gone.

The repeat flowering and deeply scented David Austin rose, 'The Squire'

David Austin roses

Winter is the best time of the year to buy rose bushes, when the major growers and nurseries sell bare-rooted plants. It's also the time to prune spring-flowering roses. These include the modern hybrid tea roses, the cluster-flowered floribundas and the David Austin roses that have the shape and scent of heritage roses, but the tough repeat-flowering characteristics of modern roses. While most roses bloom on new growth, some flower on second-year wood, or on growth from the previous season. So, take care! Many of the once-blooming old-fashioned roses are pruned *after* flowering, in most climates in late November. Don't prune too early if you live in a frost-prone climate, as you don't want the plant to shoot too soon, when there is a risk of damage to fresh young growth.

25 July

Frosty designs

Among the unexpected joys of winter are, perhaps, the pictures created by early morning frost. Even the most humble foliage and flowers become beautiful, fragile works of art when outlined in crisp white: distinctive hips that hang on to roses through winter, the bright berries of holly (*Ilex* spp.) and spindle plant (*Euonymus europaeus*), and even the foliage of lamb's ear (*Stachys lanata*). Frost clinging to delicate seed heads or plumes of grass creates an inspiring winter wonderland. Frosts are also welcomed for halting the progress of weeds and signalling a break from some of the more repetitive garden chores.

Some plants need protection from frost, however, including tomatoes, which should be swathed in plastic that is wrapped around four bamboo stakes in areas of late spring frosts. In China and Japan, the trunks of tender plants are swaddled in hessian or straw, the wrapping itself a work of art. It is possible to create igloos woven from prunings and line them with bracken, and then position them over delicate plants, to give them extra protection.

Plants such as light-coloured winter-flowering camellias can be damaged when the dawn sunshine hits frost on their blooms, which will then appear to have been burned black. At Jimbour, a large grazing property on Queensland's Darling Downs, until an automatic watering system that protected the treasured garden from frost damage was installed in the 1950s, an alarm would sound to alert household staff when an early morning frost hit, and they would rise to water away the potentially damaging ice.

26 July

Bougainvilleas

In warm temperate climates, many of the bougainvilleas will be spot-flowering, muscling up for their major performances through spring and summer. Native to Brazil, this climber was named for the French admiral Louis de Bougainville, who introduced the genus to his countrymen in 1768. The plant can be thuggish, though: the two most common species, *Bougainvillea spectabilis* and *B. glabra*, can become monsters in no time at all. In courtyards and smaller city gardens, consider using the dwarf 'Bambino' varieties, which reach only about 4 metres. There are more than twenty plants in the range, many suited to hedging, pots and hanging baskets. *B.* 'Bambino Bilas' has red flowers; 'Bambino Arora' blooms pink to cream, 'Bambino Miski' orange, and 'Bambino Zuki' purple. You could plant them all together, for an exciting clash of colours! Bougainvilleas can be espaliered along horizontally stretched wires, or in a fan shape, on walls; they will also cascade over unsightly fences and down banks.

27 July

A venerable tree, protected and supported ...

Planet Ark

If you are wondering what all those people are doing, out and about, with fork and spade in hand, I'll tell you. Planet Ark's National Tree Day (www. treeday.planetark.com) is held annually, on the last Sunday of July. The campaign started in 1996, and has resulted in more than 12 million native trees and shrubs being planted throughout Australia. Why not get involved?

Colourful creepers

The native sarsaparilla (*Hardenbergia violacea*) will be romping up and over fences, garage roofs and any tree that is in its path: its deep-purple pea flowers illuminate late winter skies in temperate climates. It is not surprising that Georgiana Molloy, one of Australia's earliest European settlers, who, with her husband, John, established the town of Augusta, in Western Australia, loved the plant. In July 1832 she wrote home: 'In these months the Wilderness indeed begins to blossom as a Rose. The purple creeper alone has consented to being domesticated and has associated its beautiful purple flowers with a very elegant pink climbing plant from the Mauritius. … In the background is the boundless and evergreen forest'.

The native sarsaparilla (*Hardenbergia violacea*) blooms with the orange trumpet creeper (*Pyrostegia venusta*)

Herbal teas

Herbal teas are easy to make, and good for the health. They are not, initially at least, as satisfying as caffeinated tea (to which, I confess, I am addicted), but, once you are accustomed to their sometimes subtle, sometimes strong, and always idiosyncratic flavour and fragrance, you are likely to become a devotee. The fact that they are doing you so much good is an added bonus. Almost any species can be used to make a tisane, or tea—except, of course, plants that are poisonous or have been sprayed with chemicals. Among the many different leaves that are delicious steeped in boiling water and strained are lemon verbena, mint and sage. Serve them in a beautiful china cup, with a thin slice of lemon and a thimble of honey.

30 July

Ellis Rowan

The flower painter Ellis Rowan was born Marian Ellis Ryan in Victoria on this day in 1848. She travelled throughout her life, often to inhospitable and dangerous locations, including the highlands of Papua New Guinea. She is counted among the most talented of natural history artists, specialising in birds and flowers, which she often set in their natural environment. In her book *A Flower-Hunter in Queensland and New Zealand*, first published in 1898, she wrote:

> The excitement of seeking and the delight of finding rare or even unknown specimens abundantly compensated me for all difficulties, fatigue, and hardships. … It has carried me into the depths of jungles, to distant islands, to wild mountain districts, and has brought me in contact with the aboriginal races, often in peculiar circumstances.

31 July

Fuss-free plants

We are in the midst of hellebore season, when those fuss-free plants add cheer to winter days. The often-inconspicuous blooms emerge from wonderful varied foliage, and team perfectly with the other quiet achievers of the botanical world. With their flowers in a range of colours—from pure white to deep purple-black—they work well with magnolias, camellias and daphnes, and with a range of late winter bulbs, particularly grape hyacinths

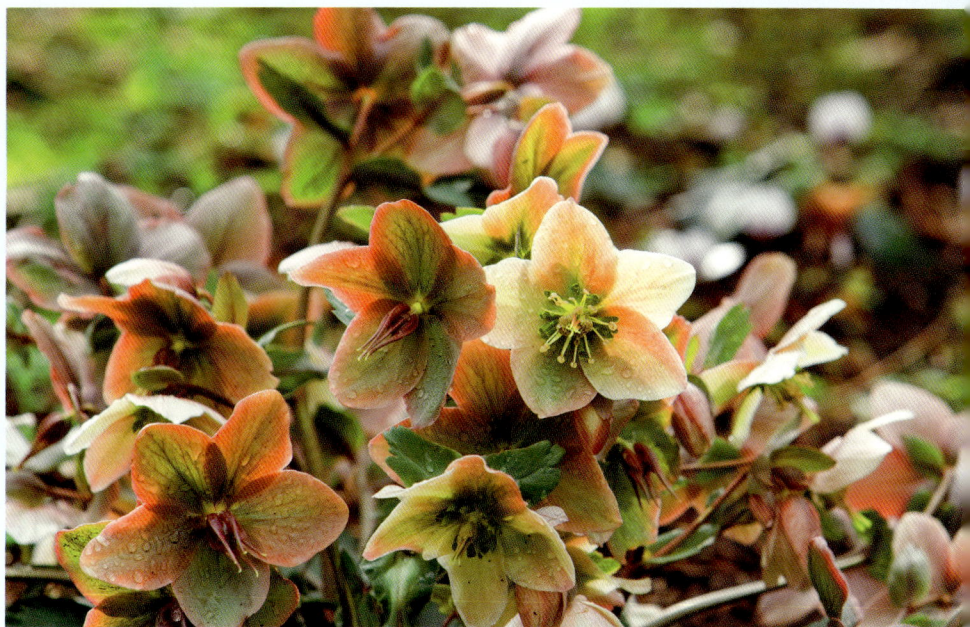

Helleborus × ericsmithii

and tulips. The most common, and easiest, hellebores to grow are the hybrids known as *Helleborus × hybridus*: these will happily multiply in anything but the poorest soil. They cope with hot summers, and with the winter rains that would rot some of the more fussy species. In September, watch for seeds forming on your hellebores: these generous performers are also somewhat promiscuous, so you must be strict with them. Don't allow to go to seed those that you don't want to cross with their neighbours.

Hellebores are charming arranged in a vase: immediately after picking, plunge the stems into boiling water to prevent the flowers from dropping. Or, pick blooms with about 10 millimetres of stem, and float them in a bowl so you can appreciate the delicate and diverse markings on their sweet, upturned faces.

Hellebores can be extremely toxic to some people: touching the seeds, or even simply the leaves, of this innocent-looking plant can cause anaphylactic reactions, including painful dermatitis. Some (perhaps all) species contain the toxic glucoside helleborin, which can cause acute reactions if touched or ingested: another reason to always wear gloves in the garden.

August

Magnificent magnolias

When the first weekend in August arrives, and the magnolias have started to flower, you are likely to proclaim them your favourite. They bloom first in warm temperate climates, and then in the colder regions west of the Great Dividing Range, and in the mountain areas. There are so many glorious magnolias, it is difficult to be disciplined about your choice. There is 'San Jose', 'Caerhays Surprise' and 'Wada's Snow White', the latter named for Koichiro Wada, who bred many magnolias at his nursery at Numazu in Japan. (When Wada realised that Japan was intending to enter World War II, he sent seeds, and specimens, of his most precious plants to horticultural friends around the world, among them *Rhododendron yakushimanum*, with its pink buds which open in spring to reveal pure-white, bell-shaped flowers.)

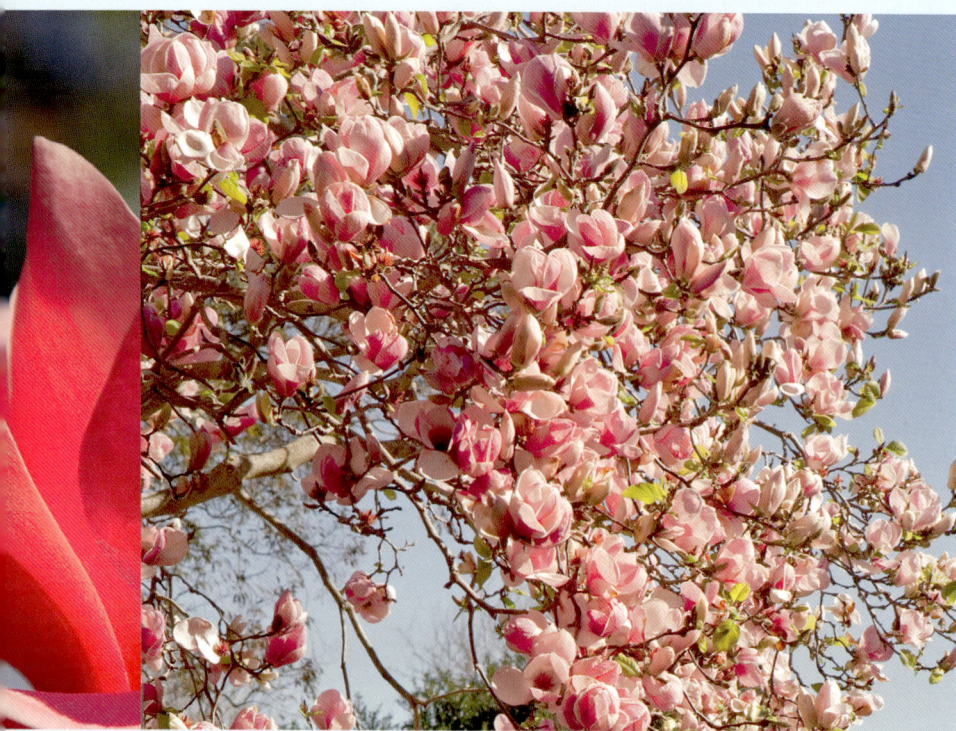

Magnolia soulangiana 'San Jose', photographed at Paradise Plants, Kulnura, New South Wales

The first of the magnolias to bloom is *Magnolia × soulangiana*, whose pink flowers look beautiful against a clear, blue winter sky; it is followed by the pure white of *M. denudata* (formerly known as *M. heptapeta*).

September is the month that the many of the late-flowering cultivars show off: *M. × soulangiana* 'Alexandrina' blooms, with large, somewhat pointed, raspberry-splashed goblets, through much of the month. It looks marvellous with burgundy and black tulips flowering around it. The cream-to yellow-flowering *M.* 'Elizabeth' also blooms late. The related port wine magnolia (*Michelia figo*) flowers in early summer.

2 August

The brassicas

It's time to feed winter vegetables, including the brassicas—cauliflowers, brussels sprouts and broccoli—with a soluble fertiliser. And it's time to plant out herbs and beans. You can sow bean seeds directly into the soil, or, if you live in a frost-prone area, allow them to germinate first in seed trays left in a warm, protected spot. Soak the seeds overnight before planting. Water well at planting time, and then not again until the seedlings appear. Also, prepare the soil for the planting of summer vegetables, particularly tomatoes (by adding lime to the soil), which can go in after the threat of frost has passed.

3 August

Weeds

Most gardeners know that weeds can escape into the natural environment, smothering, or preventing the regeneration of, native species. It is estimated that weeds cost the agricultural industry some $4 billion annually. Environmental weeds are most often introduced plants: such species include agapanthus, cape daisy, freesias and the camphor laurel, among many more. However, some native species, including several wattles, are also on the nuisance list. A recent initiative of the horticultural industry and the Australian Government, the Grow Me Instead campaign, has been devised to recommend to gardeners more sustainable plant choices. The campaign also assists nurseries in each state in advising customers on plant choices as alternatives to species that are invasive. A brochure has been produced for each Australian state and territory, providing safe choices for garden makers. In the brochure devised for New South Wales, for instance, the Cocos palm (*Syagrus romanzoffiana*) is on the 'do not plant' list, while the cabbage palm (*Livistona australis*) is among several palms recommended as safe alternatives.

But a plant that is classed as a weed in one area is not necessarily a weed in all parts of the country, or in other parts of the world. The camphor laurel (*Cinnamomum camphora*), for example, is a weed in Australia, as it contains dozens of toxic compounds, and is easily spread by birds to choke out native species, but it is popular as a street tree in much of southern China, where it is seen as a tough, pollution-tolerant and shade-giving plant.

Considered a weed in Australia, the camphor laurel is used to great effect in China.

4 August

Roberto Burle Marx

The landscape architect Roberto Burle Marx was born in São Paolo, Brazil, on this day in 1909. He implemented his first landscaping project in 1932, and became one of the most important garden designers of the twentieth century, as well as a gifted singer, jeweller, painter and sculptor. Perhaps foreshadowing the work of designers such as James van Sweden and Piet Oudolf, who plant in great masses, among the Burle Marx design innovations was the notion that species should be planted in volumes: he liked to use just one type of plant, or a single colour. 'A garden is a complex of aesthetic and plastic intentions,' he wrote in *The Christian Science Monitor* in 1986 'and the plant is, to a landscape artist, not only a plant—rare, unusual, ordinary, or doomed to disappearance—but it is also a colour, a shape, a volume, or an arabesque in itself'. Roberto Burle Marx died on 4 June 1994, having donated to the State, almost a decade earlier, his large estate and plant collection, located on the outskirts of Rio de Janeiro.

5 August

Margery Fish

The English garden writer Margery Fish was born on this day in 1892. Her garden at East Lambrook Manor, in Somerset, was created with her husband, Walter, and became a mecca for those seeking inspiration for a cottage garden style, gaining fame through Margery's charming book *We Made a Garden*, first published in 1956. In the book's introduction, she wrote: 'A good bone structure must come first, with an intelligent use of evergreen plants so that the garden is always clothed, no matter what time of year. Flowers are an added delight, but a good garden is the garden you enjoy looking at even in the depths of winter'.

6 August

Violets

Violets, flowering now, their sweet-faced, purple blooms held aloft by cerise stems above deep-green leaves, remind us that we can look to nature when considering colour combinations for fashion and furnishing. While they can be a nuisance in warm temperate gardens, spreading so heartily that they smother more delicate treasures, a posy of violets makes a welcome gift. The fact that it takes a little time to pick and that a posy is somewhat fiddly to assemble makes it even more special.

7 August

The potager

Although many of us dream of, and doodle, the perfect, decorative potager, you don't need to have a large garden to grow your own vegetables. A collection of tubs, bags and pots, complete with the possibility of crop rotation, can be just as productive as an expansive fruit and vegetable garden. Each season there is more on offer in the nurseries to help us grow safe, herbicide-free fruit and vegetables, including for those who garden in small spaces.

There are plenty of herbs and vegetables that will thrive in the smallest of spaces, as long as air circulation is good. Several horticultural companies have developed small-growing varieties, including tomatoes, watermelons, chillies and cucumbers. Add a mix of ruby chard, spinach and herbs, or plant all one vegetable: the colourful heirloom kale, perhaps.

When planting in pots, change the potting mix regularly, as the fast-growing vegetables will quickly deplete the nutrients. You can also plant vegies directly into a bag of potting mix: lay the bag flat, slit along the top and make holes around the edges. Add a few holes in the base of the bag for drainage, and plant a selection of vegetables and herbs in the potting mix. Who says you can't feed a family from a small garden?

8 August

Twenty-sixth president

Often referred to as America's first conservation president, Theodore Roosevelt established hundreds of national forests, parks and wildlife reserves, covering an area that amounted to some 100 million hectares. Elected twenty-sixth president of the United States in 1901, Roosevelt wrote, in *Outdoor Pastimes of an American Hunter*, originally published in 1905:

> It is entirely in our power as a nation to preserve large tracts of wilderness … as playgrounds for rich and poor alike … But this end can only be achieved by wise laws and by a resolute enforcement of the laws. Lack of such legislation and administration will result in harm to all of us, but most of all harm to the nature lover who does not possess vast wealth.

Gardening in small spaces—you can grow your herbs and some vegies in pots.

He signed the Antiquities Act in 1906, under which the Grand Canyon was declared a National Monument in 1908.

Roosevelt came from a family of public-spirited conservationists. His father, the philanthropist Theodore Roosevelt Snr, founded the American Museum of Natural History in 1869, having donated the land, in New York, for the museum.

A prunus bursts into flower in late winter.

August blossom

It's time to plant fruit trees. If you garden in a confined space, seek out small-growing varieties, such as the 'Angel Peach', which is perfectly happy in warm temperate climates, and 'Ballerina', or 'Tinkerbell', the dwarf form of the delicious 'Pink Lady' apple, which is self-pollinating and will grow in temperate climates, areas with a lower number of cold days than is normally required for good fruiting.

10 August

The golden dollar bush

In the sub-tropical to warm temperate parts of the country, the golden dollar bush (*Reinwardtia indica*) will be illuminating winter skies, flowering with its showy blooms. Native to northern India and a member of the flax family, this easy-going plant is happy in sun or dappled shade and doesn't demand rich soil. Comprising only two species, and native to South and South-East Asia, the plant was named for Caspar Georg Carl Reinwardt, a nineteenth-century Dutch botanist who served as the founder and first director of agriculture of the botanic garden at Bogor (then Buitenzorg), in Java, at the time a Dutch colony.

Strawberry parfait ice cream

2 or 3 punnets strawberries, roughly chopped
3 eggs, separated
pinch salt
½ cup caster sugar
600 ml cream
2 tablespoons sugar
1 teaspoon vanilla essence

Beat egg whites with salt until stiff. Add caster sugar and beat to glossy peaks. In a separate bowl, whip cream with 1 tablespoon sugar and vanilla essence. Over a double boiler, beat egg yolks with 1 tablespoon sugar until light and thick. Cool slightly and very slowly fold into cream mixture. Fold in egg whites and then strawberries. Pour into two cake tins. Freeze for 1 hour, then spoon back into bowl and beat lightly. Pour back into cold cake tins and re-freeze. Serves six.

12 August ✺

At Tari Pass, in the Southern Highlands of Papua New Guinea

The ha-ha wall

A ha-ha is a boundary that you don't see. It was invented by William Kent—who, with 'Capability' Brown and Humphry Repton, formed a triumvirate of great seventeenth- and eighteenth-century English landscapers—and first built at Levens Hall in England's Lake District. An extremely useful invention for a country garden, a ha-ha is, basically, a ditch retained by a wall, which allows a view across the landscape without the vista being interrupted by a wall or fence. At Cottesbrooke Hall, in Northampton, the North Country Mule sheep can graze peacefully within the garden picture, but safely excluded—by the ha-ha—from the precious plantings.

The ha-ha wall at Cottesbrooke allows the sheep to remain in the garden picture.

Elizabeth Macarthur

It is thought that Elizabeth Macarthur was born—in the village of Bridgerule in south-west England—on this day in 1766. The first educated woman to migrate to the colony of New South Wales, she arrived at Port Jackson on board the *Neptune*, with the Second Fleet, on 28 June 1790, with her husband, John, and baby son Edward. Elizabeth and John founded the sheep industry in Australia, first at Elizabeth Farm, at Parramatta, and then at the grand Camden Park, completed in 1836, a property that remains occupied by their descendants. The garden at Elizabeth Farm, now reconstructed to its 1830s incarnation, remains a relic of Elizabeth's ambition to succeed in her new environment. The garden must also have provided Elizabeth with comfort and solace, for she spent many years without her husband, who was twice exiled from the colony. She also suffered the death of two infants, and lived for long periods of time without several of her children, who returned at young ages to England for their education.

15 August

Birdsong

Can you imagine anything more enchanting then being woken each day by a chorus of birds? Apart from other environmental considerations, morning birdsong is among the bonuses of designing your garden with native plants, and of eschewing the use of harmful chemicals. As well, native plants bring butterflies and provide a safe haven for native fauna, creating nesting, and hiding, places.

While the rainbow lorikeet is considered something of a pest in some states, this colourful native bird adds to the morning chorus.

A single garden of local plants in any suburb will not necessarily attract a chorus of local birds, however, so some gardeners are encouraging neighbours to 'go native', in order to create a wildlife corridor. Even a few indigenous plants will help to create a safe and attractive avenue for local birds and animals, as well as creating a local vernacular look to the area. And the orchestra of song created by dozens of possible species of native birds will be a just reward.

16 August

The jade vine

If you travel in the north of Australia, watch out for our largest butterfly, the Cairns birdwing (*Ornithoptera euphorion*), fluttering around the flamboyant jade vine (*Strongylodon macrobotrys*). While native to the Philippines, the jade vine flowers from late July to November in the far north of Australia. The gorgeous blue to green vine, which bears long racemes that hang like a heavy curtain, is also greatly loved by the sunbird, familiar to gardeners in tropical Australia, which also loves the honey in the little kurrajong (*Brachychiton bidwillii*). The male sunbird has an iridescent-blue throat that contrasts with its brilliant-yellow chest.

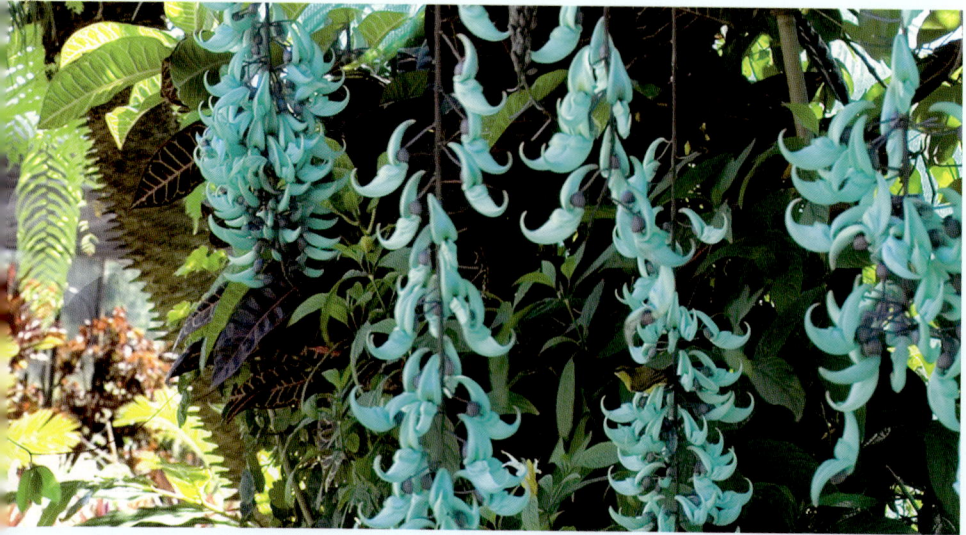

The brilliant jade vine is loved by native birds.

Generous orchids

With their thousands of species and hybrids, their often fragile form and delicate markings, and their wonderful fragrance, it is easy to understand why orchids attract the most fanatical of collectors. While the big bold cymbidiums fill nurseries and flower markets during winter, and the delicate butterfly-like phalaeonopsis inspire passionate followers, it is surely our native orchids that are the most fascinating. Many are flowering now. Some, such as *Dendrobium speciosum*, bloom in flamboyant, fragrant trusses; this glorious orchid thrives in east-facing positions, in the wild attaching itself to sandstone rocks. Others, like the tiny ironbark orchid (*D. aemulum*), flower with delicate feather-like inflorescences.

The reliable and easy *Brassia verrucosa* blooms in late winter.

Winter scale

It's important to be alert during winter for the first signs of scale on shrubs, including magnolias, michelias and camellias: you'll recognise it by the small white or grey scales attached to stems of plants. Spray with a horticultural oil such as eco-oil. There is some evidence that tipping coffee grinds onto the soil around the plants, and spraying foliage with a coffee solution, also helps. I'm trying it! At least, I've noticed that snails and slugs seem to dislike the grinds.

19 August

Plant hunters

Rhododendron arboreum subsp. *delavayi*—named after the French Catholic priest and plant hunter Jean-Marie Delavay—is native to the lower altitudes of China and so will flower, through winter, in warm temperate climates. It produces huge trusses of red, funnel-shaped blooms, from long leaves that are backed with indumentum.

20 August

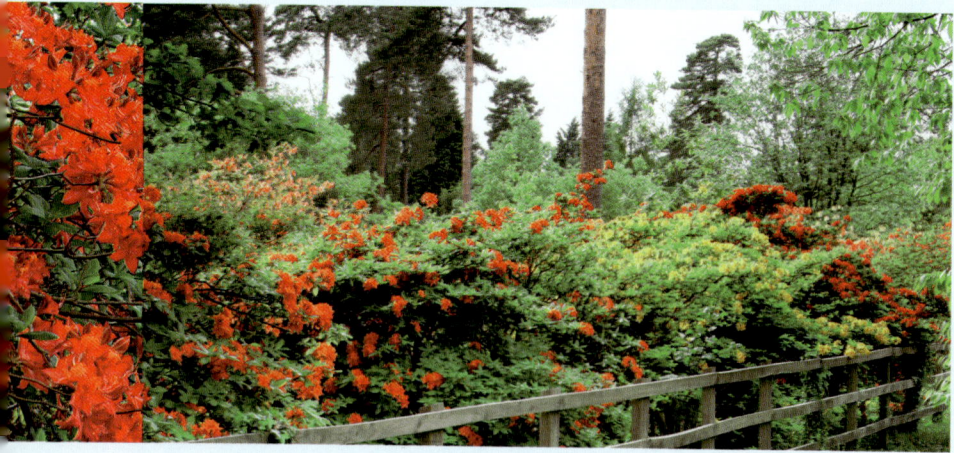

Planted en masse, gloriously coloured azaleas make an easy hedge.

Colour flash

In Australia it is still officially winter, but in the warm temperate parts of the country the promise of spring will be in the air. And in Sydney the azaleas will be in full flight: massed displays along roadsides and in gardens have to be admired, whether you like or loathe them. Spray azaleas in your garden for petal blight at the first sign of colour in the buds, and clean up under the plants so that the fungal spores do not infect the soil, to create problems in following years.

You cannot be gloomy when the golden penda blooms …

21 August

Winter cheer

If you live in warmer, frost-free parts of Australia, you will be enjoying the large yellow, cluster-like blooms of the golden penda (*Xanthostemon chrysanthus*), which flowers through winter and spring. It thrives down to the mid-north coast of New South Wales. The genus name derives from the Greek word for golden thread or stamen. The golden penda reaches to about 15 metres, and loves moisture. Clivias—although popular for their tolerance of dry shade—flowering in orange, tangerine, peach or pale yellow, look stunning when teamed with it as a ground cover.

22 August

Designing with hedges

Hedges are surely the most useful of garden design features. They provide privacy, they divide space, and, clipped low, they define areas in a garden. There is an enormous range of species that can be successfully employed as hedges. The fig (*Ficus* spp.) genus is popular for hedges, although it must be forced to behave itself: its roots, if allowed to romp away, will head for water!

Hill's weeping fig (*F. hillii*) creates a fast-growing screen, but needs to be ruthlessly pruned to keep it in check. The *Robinia* 'Mop Top' can be used instead, although it can, in some environments, sucker in a most irritating way. Either can be used, also, to create a stilt hedge, dividing the garden into compartments, while allowing tantalising glimpses of what lies beyond.

Plants belonging to the large *Hebe* genus, tough and water-wise, make excellent low hedges, and tolerate humidity better than the traditional box. For late summer colour, choose 'Purple Queen' or 'Alicia Amherst', stunning with 'White Gem' or *H. albicans*, perhaps embracing a mass of agapanthus: remember to use the sterile varieties that won't spread to become garden escapes.

Hedges add structure to gardens, formal and informal.

Tropical gardens, with their strong colours, patterns and forms, benefit from the cool, green backdrop of a hedge. In frost-free climates, and if you don't want your life ruled by the hedge trimmer, you can plant a loose hedge of the tall-growing red-leaved canna; add a second layer of interest with the shorter ginger lily (*Hedychium greenei*), with its burgundy-backed leaves. Remember, in tropical gardens, where rainfall is heavy, regular fertilising is necessary, every two to four weeks.

Tulips

The first of the tulips will have appeared by now. In warm temperate climates, treat them as an annual indulgence; even in cold climates the flower size will diminish over the years—unless, of course, you lift, fertilise and store the bulbs each year. Tulips have a long and fascinating history. In sixteenth-century Holland, collectors became so obsessed with them that they paid huge sums of money for a single bulb, some bankrupting themselves for their horticultural passion.

Tulips bloom in a civic park in Beijing.

24 August

Mamu Rainforest Walkway

After a decade in the making, the Mamu Rainforest Canopy Walkway was opened on this day in 2008. Set in the Wooroonooran National Park, in Queensland, an area of cultural significance for the Mamu people, the walkway offers spectacular views over the North Johnstone River and, beyond, to rainforest-clad mountains. There are more than 1000 metres of ground-level walking tracks, and an elevated walkway, cantilever and tower, high in the canopy of this World Heritage–listed tropical rainforest and Wet Tropics area.

25 August

Mangoes

No fruit reminds me more of summer holidays than the wonderfully scented, delicious and nutritious mango. If you live in warm or tropical climates, you may consider buying a mango tree (*Mangifera indica*), native to South-East Asia. The trees grow to around 24 metres, and develop broad canopies. Among the large-growing varieties are 'Kensington Pride', the well-known, smooth-fleshed fruit once known simply as 'Bowens'. Mangoes are self-pollinating, but will not fruit well south of Coffs Harbour, in New South Wales; they usually fruit properly in every second year. There are small-growing varieties of mango available, including 'Elwyn'. For sheltered courtyards, consider growing them in pots.

26 August

Renovate that lawn!

During the cold days of winter, it is perhaps easy to turn a blind eye to a less than perfect lawn. Spring will soon be upon gardeners in many parts of the country, however: it's time, therefore, to think about lavishing some tender care upon your lawn. Correct mowing, aerating and fertilising are all parts of a necessary maintenance program.

The first step in lawn rejuvenation is the ritual of aerating, which can be a simple matter of raking up fallen leaves. You can also pierce the lawn with a garden fork, walk on it with those spikes that attach to your shoes, or, if you are really keen, hire an aerating machine from a hardware store—watching out for any underground watering systems, and electrical cables. Next, broadcast fertiliser on the lawn when it is damp—preferably in the morning. (You may want to use a soil-wetting agent before this to assist with nutrient and moisture up-take.) Specific lawn fertilisers are readily available, or you can use Dynamic Lifter; a slow-release organic conditioner is best. Water in fertiliser, as always, after applying.

Watch out for weeds such as bindii in growing lawns, once the warm weather arrives. Use lawn weeder, or a 'weed and feed' product suitable for your type of grass; with all species, apply this before seed sets. Lawn pests that are out and about now include the black beetle, whose larva is the dreaded curl grub. Treat it with a low-toxic, synthetic pyrethroid: it won't enter the food chain and is not harmful to earthworms and other useful soil organisms.

27 August

Crab-apples

In cool and temperate climates, many members of the Rosaceae family will be flowering now, among them the crab-apples. One of the loveliest of deciduous trees for cold-climate gardens, the crab-apple is a member of

Crab-apples make a smart entrance—here, *Malus floribunda.*

the *Malus* genus, which contains around thirty species of fruiting and non-fruiting trees. The most common is, of course, the eating apple (*M. pumila)*, but many will agree that the crab-apple is the most elegant of the genus.

Mainly small- to medium-size trees native to the cooler countries of the Northern Hemisphere, crab-apples are beautiful over many months, with delicate blossom in spring, a parade of bright fruits and brilliant autumn foliage. A smart entrance can be formed by a pair of *M. floribunda* (the first of the crab-apples to flower) standing sentinel at a gate. This species, which also copes with warmer climates throughout Australia, blooms with masses of hot-pink buds that open to a softer pink. Perhaps the most charming of all the species is the Iowa crab-apple (*M. ioensis)*: the downy, apple-green leaves that emerge at the end of winter are followed by dark-pink flower buds that unfurl into refined shell-pink blossoms. A small, neat tree that grows well in warm temperate climates away from the coast, it is recognised by its layered branches that descend to the ground in beautiful horizontal sweeps. The only pruning desirable is the removal of inner branches that are crossing or, through incorrect pruning, shooting upwards.

M. × *purpurea* 'Eleyi' has arresting purple leaves, crimson flowers and red fruit, while its cousin *M.* 'Aldenhamensis' flowers wine red up to three times in a season and has purple fruit. Among the most scented are the flowers of the American sweet crab-apple (*M. coronaria*), although the fruit is bitter. The southern crab-apple (*M. angustifolia*) and *M. bracteata* are also very fragrant: plant them where the prevailing winds will carry the scent to the house.

28 August

Martin Luther King

Barack Obama formally accepted the US Democrat Party's nomination to run for president on this day in 2008. He delivered his acceptance speech in Denver, Colorado, where the state flower, the Rocky Mountains columbine (*Aquilegia caerulea*), was blooming. The fact that Obama gave his address on the forty-fifth anniversary of Martin Luther King's 'I Have a Dream' speech made the occasion all the more poignant. King spoke from the Lincoln Memorial, Washington, DC, where, at the height of that summer in 1963, the *Magnolia grandiflora* would have been a mass of cream, scented goblets. In the warm temperate parts of Australia, the *M. grandiflora* 'Little Gem', a smaller growing cultivar of the big bull bay magnolia, will still be flowering now.

And today is Daffodil Day throughout Australia: the millions of dollars raised annually in this Cancer Council campaign go towards research, support services and education.

29 August

The torch ginger

While those in southern states continue to shiver through winter, in the tropical north the torch gingers (*Etlingera elatior*) will be blooming, adding an exotic tone to gardens that bask in the sun. Native to tropical Asia, the plant's flowers erupt from underground rhizomes, and bloom on statuesque stems that can reach 3 metres in height. The edible, red, waxy bracts—the pink is rare—are arranged around a head of imbricated petals, each of which is outlined with a fine, white line. The torch ginger likes well-drained, rich soil and flourishes in sun, or part shade. Deadhead for continuous blooming, and propagate by dividing the rhizomes in the warm months.

30 August

Marianne North

The English flower painter Marianne North died on this day in 1890. Born at Hastings, on 24 October 1830, North turned to flower painting after she realised she was not talented enough to become a professional singer, often painting while travelling with her father, the member of parliament for Hastings. After his death, in 1869, she decided to paint the flora of foreign countries and, in 1871, set out for Canada, the United States, and Jamaica, living for a year in a hut in the forests of Brazil. From 1875, she travelled the world, painting—with exacting scientific accuracy—the flora of Tenerife, California, Japan, Borneo, Java, India and Ceylon, now Sri Lanka. Inspired by Charles Darwin's enthusiasm for the antipodes, North travelled to Australia and New Zealand in 1880. Upon her return to England her work was presented to the Royal Botanic Gardens at Kew, with a purpose-built gallery to house the collection opened in 1882.

31 August

Spring is coming!

Winter is drawing to a close. You may find this difficult to believe if you live in our southern states, which can experience cold days, and nights, for several more weeks. In the warmer parts of the country, though, spring is definitely in the air, and the wisterias are preparing for their annual performance. (In the colder areas of the country, and in mountain regions, you will have to wait until mid October for wisteria blooms, keeping your fingers crossed that late spring frosts will not burn those promising, plump buds.) If you haven't yet pruned your roses, do it today!

September

The 'King Alfred' daffodil

1 September

Happiness is …

Happiness is an armful of daffodils! While spring doesn't officially start until 22 September, many of us feel that the new season is here when the first day of September arrives. The spring bulbs are flowering: after the snowdrops and narcissuses of mid winter, the bluebells are out, and the tulips are emerging from the soil. Borders and fields are awash with daffodils.

Today is National Wattle Day: many wattles in the southern states of Australia flower this month, although others bloom through July and August. The golden wattle (*Acacia pycnantha*) was proclaimed our national flower in 1988 (although, along with the Cootamundra wattle (*A. baileyana*), it is also on the weeds list). Some, like the cinnamon wattle (*A. leprosa*), are red-flowered; others, such as the fringed wattle (*A. fimbriata*), are low-growing, and love being clipped into shape; and the fan wattle (*A. amblygona*) makes a terrific ground cover. *A. verticillata* provides a great refuge for small native birds. Wattles are particularly useful in landscaping as nursery trees; fast-growing but short-lived, they provide protection for slow-growing, more precious trees. By the time these trees can stand safely alone, the wattles will have reached the end of their lives.

2 September

Spring showers

Spring can bring showers, as the song says, so it is time to fertilise, to assist new growth. Clean out fireplaces and fire boxes, and spread the ash around roses. Lightly feed tall bearded irises, which are getting ready for an early summer show: they love the same conditions and fertilisers as roses, so the two are often planted together. Remember, irises like to be planted with their rhizomes at soil level, and in climates where the frost can bite and the sun can burn. When flowering is over, cut the leaves back, feed and mulch, taking care not to cover the rhizomes.

3 September

Weedbusters week

It's Weedbusters Week! Held over seven days in early September, and the culmination of the year-long program of weed awareness, Weedbusters Week (www.weedbusters.info) is a community initiative aimed at educating the public about responsible land management. It began in 1994 as Queensland Weed Awareness Week and in 1997 became a national event, with the support of the federal and state governments, along with the Cooperative Research Centre for Australian Weed Management.

4 September

Staking trees

While September is a month of excitement and anticipation, we can be fooled by all that colour and scent into thinking the cold weather is over. Chill winds can hit suddenly, however, just when we thought it was time to pack away the winter woollies. So, if you subscribe to the tree-staking view, make sure that young trees are well staked now. I like to provide some help to trees during their formative years, even though some gardeners believe they should be left to fend for themselves, developing strong roots to withstand the onslaught of annual winds. I use three or four stakes—timber or galvanised iron posts—and secure the young tree with a wide hessian ribbon, or plastic strap, wrapped around the trunk and each stake in a figure of eight, until it is established. For copses of young trees I erect a shelter barrier of shade cloth tensioned across several star posts—just for the few weeks when I know that the winds can suddenly arrive.

5 September

'My country'

Dorothea Mackellar, the author of the poem 'My Country', read it publicly for the first time on this day in 1905, in London. It has since become a national anthem for many Australians.

6 September

Tree dahlias

Tree dahlias (*Dahlia imperialis*), shrubs native to South America that reach some 5 metres, will be starting to shoot. Cut back old canes and use them to grow new plants: divide them into pieces with at least two sets of nodes, and lay them flat in a trench. Cover with soil and replant after the new growth has emerged.

7 September

Royal Botanic Gardens

In Sydney's Royal Botanic Gardens—surely the world's best located public garden—spring arrives in a flurry of scent and colour. A mecca for garden lovers, who visit to find beauty, learning and peace, the gardens are located at Farm Cove, on the site where the first farm was established after European settlement, by Captain Arthur Phillip, in 1788. The gardens were founded in 1816 by Governor Lachlan Macquarie, but Charles Moore, director from 1848 to 1896, is credited with developing them to their present form. As you would expect in a garden of some 30 hectares, several visits are needed to appreciate everything that grows there. This week, in the Spring Walk, the vibrant colours of thousands of tulips will be cooled by swathes of *Osmanthus delavayi* and May bush (*Spiraea cantoniensis*), blooming in fragrant clouds of white. Above, an avenue of peach will soon unfurl its pink, white and red blooms.

The spring border at Sydney's Royal Botanic Gardens

8 September

Propagating frangipani

Now is the time to take hardwood cuttings from a range of trees, including the jacaranda and frangipani. To propagate the latter, take cuttings up to 50 centimetres in length. Leave them in the open air for up to a week so that the cut end can dry out, forming a callus, and preventing fungal infection. Then, pot them up in potting mix or plant them straight into the ground: stake well, as the roots are slow to form and the plant will be top-heavy. Take care with frangipani: the milky sap that seeps from cut branches, or when leaves are removed, is poisonous, and can damage the eyes and cause skin irritations.

9 September

Garden festivals

It's time for garden shows and expositions. The Mount Macedon Horticulture Society holds the marvellous Plant Lovers' Market (www.mtmacedonhort .org.au/events/plantlovers) east of Melbourne each spring.

In Canberra, Floriade (www.floriadeaustralia.com), a huge flower festival, is held from mid September to early October, and includes show gardens and workshops. On the Southern Highlands of New South Wales, Bowral's Tulip Time is celebrated during the last week in September and the first week of October. Central to the festivities is a massed display of 100 000 tulips and 25 000 annuals in Corbett Gardens. Private gardens also open their gates, and there are tours and talks, a street fair, and window displays.

10 September

Nancy Lancaster

The American Nancy Perkins Field Tree Lancaster was born on this day in 1897, at Mirador, her grandfather's majestic estate in Virginia, a Federal house, built in 1825, and surrounded by glorious gardens. After her mother died, the young Nancy spent a great deal of time in England, with her aunt Nancy, Viscountess Astor, the first woman to become a member of parliament. After her second marriage, in 1920, to Ronald Tree, Nancy settled in New York, returning often, during spring and autumn, to Mirador.

After returning to England, in 1944 Nancy bought the interior design firm of Colefax and Fowler, which, across the world, has come to epitomise, perhaps, an English 'country house' style. Cecil Beaton, in *The Glass of Fashion*, published in 1954, noted that Nancy had a talent for 'sprucing up a stately but shabby home and making a grand house appear less grand'.

Nancy employed Russell Page and Geoffrey Jellicoe, among the world's most important twentieth-century garden writers and landscapers, in several of the gardens she owned in England. One was Ditchley Park, in Oxfordshire; the garden had been laid out in 1726 by James Gibbs, and altered by 'Capability' Brown in the 1760s, and again by John Claudius Loudon between 1805 and 1810. Page and Jellicoe extended the original terraces to acknowledge the surrounding landscape, shaped the hedges and added important ornamentation.

11 September

Summer vegie planting

Each year, since 2001, I have planted out my summer vegetables on 11 September. On that day, it was therapeutic to be putting something good into the soil, to be planning the nutritious things that would come from that soil in a few months. The planting came to signify beauty emerging from ugliness, light from dark. So, in temperate climates, plant a selection of tomatoes (you will plant more over the next couple of months to ensure an ongoing supply), along with some chillies, eggplants, beans and peas, and a variety of lettuces. Members of the Curcurbitaceae family, which includes melons, pumpkins, cucumbers and zucchini, can also go in now, and over the next six weeks.

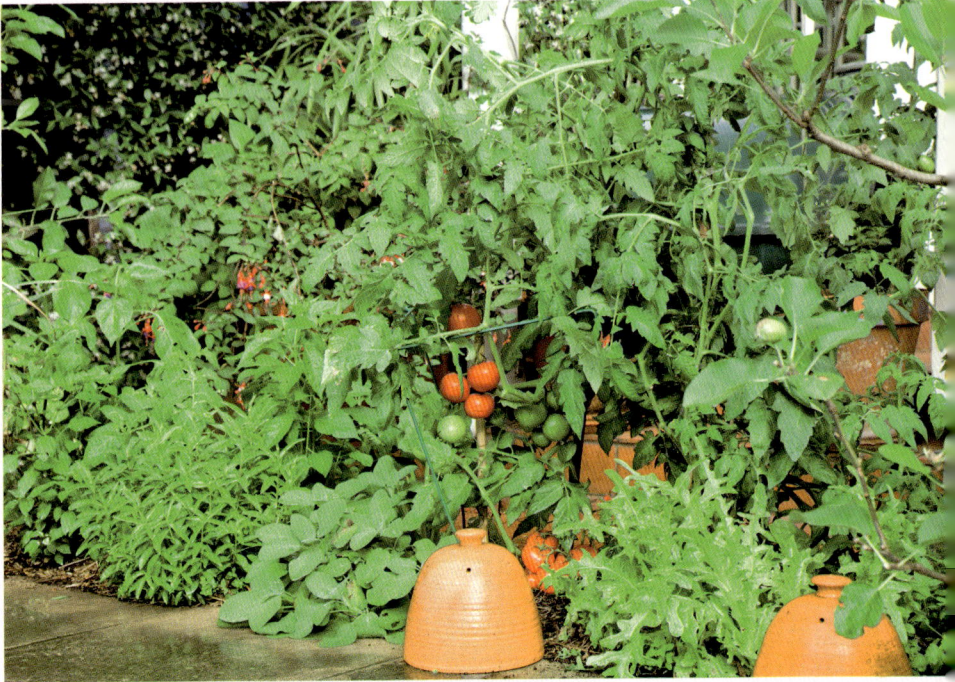

In warm temperate climates tomatoes planted now will bear fruit during summer.

Chillies like the same conditions as tomatoes. I like to plant the two side by side, and often use them together in cooking. When preparing soil for tomatoes, dig in a little calcium to combat any deficiency that will encourage an unsightly brown patch to develop from the flower end of the fruit: not surprisingly, this is known as blossom-end rot.

Plant snow and sugar snap peas, in a sunny spot, into a friable soil that has been well prepared with composted manure. Go easy on the nitrogen-rich fertiliser; they need potassium and phosphorus to fruit well. They will take between twelve and fifteen weeks to grow, from planting to harvest.

12 September

Port Fairy Festival

Port Fairy, west of Melbourne, is one of the prettiest places in the country; it's a picture-postcard town of some 2500 inhabitants and dozens of historic, listed buildings. It was established as a whaling base before developing into a thriving coastal and river port; today, it also hosts a busy calendar of cultural events, from book fairs to music festivals. Its annual Ex Libris writers' festival (www.exlibris.port-fairy.com), held this month, includes garden writers and conservationists; as well, several excellent gardens are open to visitors. Among the many interesting sessions for gardening enthusiasts are presentations on climate change, dry gardens, permaculture and sustainable living.

If you take the Great Ocean Road to the town, you'll pass the Twelve Apostles, strange pieces of rock that stand, glowering, in an often wild sea. En route is the Otway Fly treetop walk, which winds through a high canopy of cool temperate rainforest of mountain ash, blackwood and beech myrtle.

13 September

Lawns

You've probably renovated your lawn, but, as the weather warms, the weeds emerge. Take care not to cut the lawn too low at this time of the year: known as scalping, it will expose the soil, which will encourage weeds. Mow before any weeds have time to seed and treat with weed killer. It is possible to counter broad-leaf lawn weeds by sprinkling onto them a mixture of one cup each of washed sand, potassium sulphate (potash) and iron sulphate.

Be alert also for the dreaded onion weed, or oxalis, which must be one of the most irritating of all garden pests. You will be able to distinguish the onion weed from some of your fine-leaved bulbs by the flower heads. Snap these off before they have a chance to go to seed. Paint the strap-like leaves with a poison that contains glyphosate, such as Roundup or Zero. You may need to repaint several times. Be careful with the use of glyphosate around roses, however, as it can cause distortion in leaves and set back growth and flowering by several years. Isolate the weed in a cut-off plastic drink bottle if you need to protect surrounding plants. You can dig onion weed out if you are very careful to take a quantity of soil with it so that the tiny bulbils don't spread further.

14 September

Borage

Have you planted borage in your garden? Greatly loved by bees, which are essential for pollination of fruit, vegies, herbs and flowers, this tall-growing herb blooms in a sky blue for much of the year. Broadcast seeds across your herb and vegetable gardens, and across your flower borders, or plant up small pots. As well as the European honeybee, which was introduced to Australia in the early nineteenth century, there are some 1500 species of Australian bees. Many of these are stingless and produce honey, a popular bush food, from native plants.

15 September

Feed your citrus

Now that the peak of the citrus season is almost over, it's time to give trees a light feed of a prepared citrus food. Citrus need trace elements to ensure sweet fruit and thin skins. They also benefit from being sprayed with magnesium and zinc, available as ready-mixed powder at garden centres. (You can also use this to spray grapevines.) Spray at flushing—when the trees produce

Pots of citrus at the Villa Reale in Italy lead the eye towards distant views.

a burst of new green leaves—so that the soft young growth can absorb the spray. Remember to water well before you fertilise, and again afterwards. But citrus will not stand for bad drainage, so, if your trees are in pots, ensure that they are not sitting in a saucer of water.

16 September

Orchids of Papua New Guinea

On this day in 1975, Papua New Guinea declared full independence, with Sir Michael Somare as its first prime minister. The country's beautiful islands, with their central rib of stunning highlands, are home to thousands of species of orchid—and searching for them is a journey straight out of an adventure book.

Countless species of the *Dendrobium* genus are native to New Guinea's Southern Highlands. The epiphytic *D. hellwigianum*, which flourishes in massive clumps of humus caught in trees in high altitudes, blooms in tufts of pink-and-white inflorescences. The tiny pink-flowering *D. bracteosum* clings to the sides of tree trunks, as does the brilliant orange-and-pink *D. subclausum*. The large-flowered *D. forbesii*, which occurs high in the rainforest canopies, in decomposed organic matter caught in the trees, has clusters of white-and-lemon fragrant flowers. Another epiphyte from the area, *D. finisterrae*, has speckled brown-and-cream blooms that are covered in dense hairs: it is the hairiest flower of all the orchids! The pendant orchid (*D. geotropum*)—the species name means upside down—is found at the highest altitudes, and was described and classified by botanists only in 1986. It is normally hidden in the treetops by leaves and moss, which protect the long-lasting flowers.

Several orchids occur on the ground, in the grasslands and heathland. The grass orchids, or grastidiums, a sub-section of the *Dendrobium* genus, flourish in such areas, along with carpets of *Spathoglottis parviflora*, a small pink orchid that emerges from a sheath of pleated leaves.

The very fragrant *Coelogyne bacarrii* in Dave Kirrili's garden at Tari Pass

17 September

Poisonous plants

Many garden plants are poisonous or can cause serious reactions, from bruising and swelling of limbs, and peeling of skin, to pain and breathing difficulties. Some of the most toxic plants look quite innocent, and many are positively beguiling. It is well known, for example, that several members of the Apocynaceae family—which includes those flamboyant beauties frangipani and poinsettia—exude a milky sap that can cause severe illness and even death. Some bulbs, oleander, elephant's ear (*Alocasia* spp.), parts of the agapanthus and, of course, many fungi, are poisonous if ingested.

It seems that primulas, those dancing pretties, along with poppies and privet, can cause anaphylactic reactions. The gorgeous frilled, funnel-shaped blooms of *Primula obconica*, introduced to the west from its native China in 1880, rather conveniently goes by the common name of the poison primula. It flowers in pinks, whites and mauves, is delicately fragrant and delicious to bees, but, to us, is poisonous if eaten, and can also cause skin irritations.

A friend of mine developed an angry red rash on his arms after clearing common ivy from a garage roof. And an Australian who is a guide at the wonderful gardens of the Villa Landriana, near Rome, writes that she has noted breathing difficulties—even in people who don't usually suffer from allergies—from contact with the stunning tall-growing rice-paper plant (*Tetrapanax papyrifer*).

The lesson from these experiences is that we should always wear gloves in the garden. Try those thin rubber 'skins' under your favourite garden gloves. Along with protecting you from things that bite and sting, the skins will protect your hands from grime, which will quickly betray your horticultural passion.

18 September

Camden Park

The orchid, or butterfly, tree (*Bauhinia galpinii*) will be flowering now at Camden Park, in New South Wales, the home of Elizabeth Macarthur from 1836. It was planted there as seed by the explorer Ludwig Leichhardt, who stayed at Camden Park on several occasions. Elizabeth's son William was a respected plant collector and nurseryman, and sponsored adventurers like Leichhardt, who, in turn, sent back plants collected on his travels through the country. The garden housed treasures from botanic gardens around the world, including buddleia, clematis and ficus from Calcutta. Other rare plants still growing in the garden include the oldest camellia in Australia (*Camellia japonica* 'Anemoniflora'), first taken to England from China in 1806, and a tree gardenia (*Rothmannia globosa*) from South Africa, which is covered in fragrant cream blooms each spring.

Native birds love the nectar in *Melaleuca linariifolia*.

19 September

The paperbarks

In temperate climates, the paperbarks (*Melaleuca* spp.), which flower all through winter, will still be blooming. Among the most generous are the *M. linariifolia*, which bears white, fluffy flowers that are filled with nectar, attracting native birds and insects. The old-fashioned 'Snowstorm' is a variety that grows to about 3 metres, making it a great choice as a specimen shrub, or for hedging. It bears fresh, lime-green foliage in spring and clouds of scented white blossom. It is easy-going, too, happy in dry-ish soils, as well as in its more usual environment, water-logged areas.

20 September

Bromeliads

Bromeliads can be divided at any time of the year. Break off the 'babies', or 'pups', that appear alongside the main plant. Re-pot or plant in leaf litter or orchid mix, as they don't like having their feet in damp soil. Among the hardiest of plants (although they aren't keen on frost), bromeliads will cope with dark and shady corners. In their natural habitat in much of South America, many are epiphytes, growing in leaf litter high in trees. Many love being grown in the misty, humid atmosphere of a bathroom.

21 September

Important in a coastal garden: create a microclimate behind hedges.

Creating microclimates

Salt-laden winds can hit coastal gardens at any time of the year, but if hedges are employed to create a microclimate to protect vulnerable plants, gardens close to the sea can be most successful, and many will be blooming now. Consider a double hedge, which not only looks smart, but provides extra protection for the garden. There is a range of species available that will cope with the onslaught of sea salt and wind, including the lemon-scented myrtle (*Backhousia citriodora*), which clips to make an excellent hedge; its aromatic leaves also make a refreshing tea. Among the toughest of plants for first-tier hedging are the Indian hawthorn (*Rhaphiolepis umbellata* 'Apple Blossom'), the white-flowering *Escallonia* 'Iveyi' and the New Zealand Christmas tree (*Metrosideros excelsa*).

The coast daisy (*Olearia axillaris*) also performs well in seaside gardens, as do the versatile Australian fuchsia (*Correa reflexa*) and the sea box (*Alyxia buxifolia*).

22 September

Potting up

Today is the official start of spring. It's a busy time in the garden, with lots on the 'must do' list. It is a good time to change the potting mix in all your pots. Buy the best quality potting mix you can. Take care: always wear gloves, along with a protective mask, when handling potting mix, to ensure that you don't breathe in particles, particularly when opening the bag. Potting mix and other bagged soil, manures and compost products, along with soils and leaf litter 'in the open' contain dangerous spores of such diseases as legionnaire's.

It's also time to feed frangipani, as these glorious trees are getting ready to bud up. Use a complete fertiliser with an extra dollop of potassium sulphate to encourage flowering.

23 September

Upside down orchids

The epiphytic and vanilla-scented stanhopeas are a perfect choice for planting in hanging baskets, as they have a cascading habit. Line a basket with bark and fill a pot with pieces of the orchids and potting mix. The flowers emerge from the base of the basket, which has led to the common name for these gorgeous plants: upside down orchids.

24 September

Using bananas

Here is my daughter Olivia's recipe for banana cake, a great way to use up overripe fruit. Try sprinkling shredded coconut over the top before baking: it's delicious.

Banana cake

175 g plain flour
2 teaspoons baking powder
½ teaspoon bicarbonate of soda
125 g butter, melted
150 g caster sugar
2 large eggs
3 large, ripe bananas, mashed
1 teaspoon vanilla extract
100 g sultanas or dried apple, chopped,
soaked in boiling water to cover

Grease and lightly flour a medium-size loaf tin. Preheat oven to 180°C.
Sift together flour and baking powder in a small bowl, and stir in
bicarbonate of soda. In a large bowl mix together butter and sugar. Add
eggs, one at a time, followed by bananas and vanilla. Mix in the flour
mixture one-third at a time, and gently fold through sultanas or dried
apple. (Do not overmix.) Tip mixture into tin and cook for 60–75 minutes,
until a skewer inserted into the centre comes out clean. Remove from tin
when slightly cooled and cool further on a wire rack.

25 September

Tree ferns

It's not just the colours of spring blossom that make this season so exciting;
the soft green shoots of bulbs, the lime green of fresh, new leaves emerging
on the bare limbs of deciduous trees, and the soft unfurling fronds of ferns
can be just as energising. A combination of shapes, textures and shades is
central to the success of any garden, and among the plants that contribute to
the creation of a lush, cool tapestry of foliage is the tree fern.

Tree ferns date back 400 million years, and range from tall-growing
plants to low, delicate ground covers. They evoke images of intrepid plant
hunters risking their lives in mountain passes and dangerous jungles to
transport botanical prizes back to garden owners hungry for the rare and
unusual. They speak of elegant days past, of tea dances in palm courts and of
pink gins enjoyed in the shadowy courtyards of the Far East.

A forest of tree ferns (*Cyathea atrox*) grows in the valley of an ancient glacier, 4000 metres up Mount Wilhelm, in the Central Highlands of Papua New Guinea. The twin peaks opposite are in the Bismarck Range.

Most tree ferns are located in two genera, *Cyathea* and *Dicksonia*, and are native to the humid sub-tropical and tropical, frost-free regions of the world. An umbrella-like crown of lacy, weeping fronds, or crosiers, emanates from a central bud held atop a stem, which can reach up to 20 metres. I love the sense of renewal that these fronds, which are often covered in soft, fibrous tissue, provide as they uncurl. The stem is a complicated system of tissues which conduct nutrients to the fronds, and is often covered in brown, fibrous aerial roots. Tree ferns enjoy rainforest conditions of misted, dappled light and moist, humus-rich soil. If you grow them in your garden, they will thank you for a teaspoon of sugar, once a month, placed in the centre of the fronds, and, if your specimens have not grown too tall, water poured down the neck.

Garden sculptures add interest to Jan Todd's spring vegie garden.

26 September

Clash those colours!

Break the rules. Just as you might add a carmine ottoman or sofa to a room with golden-yellow walls, ignoring some of the conventions of interior design, you can break many of the rules of gardening. Plant vegies in flower borders, grow your broccoli—usually a winter vegetable—through summer, and prune when you get the time (though never when you might be removing flower buds). You can clash purple and yellow—or even orange—in your garden if you wish; add a hot pink if you want to be really outrageous. But, as with all such behaviour, do it in style and as if you mean it: plant in big, generous swathes.

27 September

Pavlova and passionfruit

You just can't enjoy pavlova—that wonderful concoction of meringue, ice cream, cream and fruit that epitomises the Australian summer—without passionfruit (*Passiflora edulis*). The fruit is easy to grow, too, if you have the space. It is native to South America, but is now widely grown through warm countries. Among the varieties available are 'Nelly Kelly', the best choice for temperate climates, and the hybrids 'Panama Red' or 'Panama Gold', which do well in the tropics.

Passionfruits not only taste delicious; they are also healthy, high in vitamins A and C, potassium and fibre. If you are lucky enough to have too many passionfruits, put the whole fruits in the freezer: defrosted, they taste just as good as when freshly harvested. It is said that the common name was given to the fruit by early Christian missionaries, because they associated the complex structure of the passionfruit flower with the Passion of Christ.

In warm-climate gardens, prune your passionfruit now, as it flowers and fruits in the hottest months on new wood. Cut back by a third to encourage new growth.

28 September

Landscaper Daniel Baffsky has created a rooftop garden for an apartment development in central Sydney.

Green roofs and walls

Have you ever thought about creating a green wall? You may have noticed green walls in other countries, where buildings of several storeys are sometimes covered in plant material. One way of facing today's environmental challenges, particularly climate change, green walls are created from free-standing fences and wired structures, or from walls that form part of a building. They reduce maintenance, cool buildings through living insulation, and reduce noise and run-off from stormwater. They are also aesthetically pleasing.

29 September

The Swan Lake, which was completed in 1866 in Singapore's Botanic Gardens, is shaded by a stand of the towering, slender, bamboo-like Nibung palm (*Oncosperma tigillarium*).

30 September

Pest and disease watch!

Even though spring is such a generous time in the garden—full of colour and scent, with few of the problems associated with the humidity of summer weather—it is a time to consider, and to pre-empt, some pests and diseases. A wide range of fruit is susceptible to the dreaded Queensland fruit fly. Stone fruit, mangoes, strawberries and tomatoes will all succumb if you are not vigilant. Get out the fruit fly traps now, ready to use over the warmer months. These are a monitoring tool only: they simply attract the male fruit flies to alert you to their presence in the garden. You then need to hang baits to attract and destroy the females, which, if not caught, will lay eggs, in late spring and summer, just beneath the surface of developing fruit and some vegetables. When the eggs hatch, the larvae will burrow towards the centre of the fruit.

You can make a fruit fly trap with an empty plastic drink bottle. Pierce the bottle all the way around, one-third of the way down, making medium-size holes. Mix together two tablespoons each of cloudy ammonia and sugar, half a cup of water and a few drops of a prepared fruit fly control, and pour it into the bottle. Screw on the lid and hang the bottle in the tree. Check the trap regularly for dead flies and recharge it when liquid is depleted. Also, collect and destroy any fallen fruit.

As soon as you plant tomatoes, you need to address the problem of white-fly, a sap-sucking pest. It can be controlled with parasitic wasps (*Encarsia formosa*), which can be bought by mail order. The wasps should be introduced in spring, three times, a fortnight apart each time, so that they attack the flies during their reproductive stage—they are not effective once the flies have matured, when they take flight in clouds as you approach the affected plant. At this point you need a tomato dust containing spinosaid, an insecticide derived from natural soil bacteria.

Watch out for rust spores on the emerging leaves of your frangipanis, which will cause premature leaf fall. Rust, which can also infect geraniums, is more severe in times, and areas, of high humidity. Get on to it quickly, before the spores spread and infect the entire plant: spray weekly or fortnightly with eco-oil. Destroy any infected leaves.

October

The scent of lilac ensures it has a place in a cool-climate garden.

1 October

It's lilac time

If you are away from home this month, you may find yourself dreaming of all that you are missing in your garden. In temperate climates gardens will be bursting into life: the wisteria is out, as is the first rose, and jasmine is filling the air with scent. And it's lilac time in cool-climate areas. It would be impossible not to adore these rather inauspicious shrubs that, just once each year, burst into dense panicles of highly scented florets. Best known to most gardeners is the common lilac (*Syringa vulgaris*): one of two species that hail from eastern Europe, it is resplendent for a few brief, if brilliant, weeks each year. It has around 1500 cultivars, most of which were developed in France in the late nineteenth and early twentieth centuries, and are often grafted onto the lilac's close cousin, privet (*Ligustrum* spp.), also a member of the olive family. Most of the two dozen species of lilac come from the mountainous regions of Asia, however, from Afghanistan through China to Japan. *S. pekinensis* arrived in western gardens from China in the middle of the eighteenth century, with *S. oblata*, *S. pubescens* and *S. villosa* following in the mid- to late nineteenth century; the delicate *S. meyeri* was discovered in a garden near Peking in 1909.

Lilacs flower in many shades, from the palest mauve, to the richest, most intense purple, but also in cerise and pink, white and cream. The choice includes the gorgeous white-flowered 'Mme Lemoine' and the famous blue-purple 'President Lincoln'. *S.* × *persica* is good for hedging, while *S. protolaciniata*, and its offspring, will tolerate more warmth than most species, so are suited to warm temperate climates.

2 October

Mount Annan Botanic Garden

Opened on this day in 1988, Mount Annan Botanic Garden is located at Camden, south of Sydney. The garden, which showcases over 4000 native Australian plants, and covers more than 400 hectares, includes a section of remnant Cumberland Plain Woodland, particular collections of plants that once covered a large part of the Sydney Basin. Some of the plants found in the area are native box (*Bursaria spinosa*), ironbarks, forest red gum (*E. tereticornis*) and grey box (*Eucalyptus moluccana*).

Banksia spinulosa

From the 25 000 species of plants that are native to Australia, a selection from a wide range of climates is represented at Mount Annan, from the deserts to the mountain ranges and rainforests. The botanic garden includes a banksia and grevillea garden, the Wollemi Walk of Discovery, a wattle garden, a eucalypt arboretum, and a rare and endangered plants garden. There are also walks that pass ornamental lakes, natural woodlands, forests, grasslands and unique features such as the Sundial of Human Involvement, where visitors can tell the time by the casting of their own shadow.

3 October

The renga renga lily

In warm temperate climates and coastal gardens, the renga renga lily (*Arthropodium cirratum*), native to New Zealand, will be flowering now, sending up plumes of white flowers. These great-value plants, with their gentle blue-grey foliage, make stunning low hedges; or they can drift through a border, as a rib, to add structure, or fill out beds, when planted in multiples. They do, however, attract snails and slugs, which strip the leaves in the most unsightly way. Apply snail deterrent that is friendly to pets and native fauna, or place snail pellets in plastic milk bottles or cartons to attract snails but keep other animals safe. You can also scour your garden, by torchlight after dark, after the first rains in early spring, with a bucket of hot water into which the snails can be dropped. Or, set out shallow dishes of beer to allow them to die happily drunk. Hippeastrums and clivias should be protected in the same way. Hostas, also, are caviar to these garden pests, and once the leaves are damaged they are ruined for the entire season.

4 October

Bulbs

It's time to remove spent winter-flowering bulbs. If you have tulips whose leaves have died right back, gently pull the bulbs out; store them carefully in your garden shed, protected from vermin. Next autumn, chill the bulbs in the fridge (carefully marked, of course) for several weeks before planting; augment the display by indulging in an annual purchase of fresh bulbs.

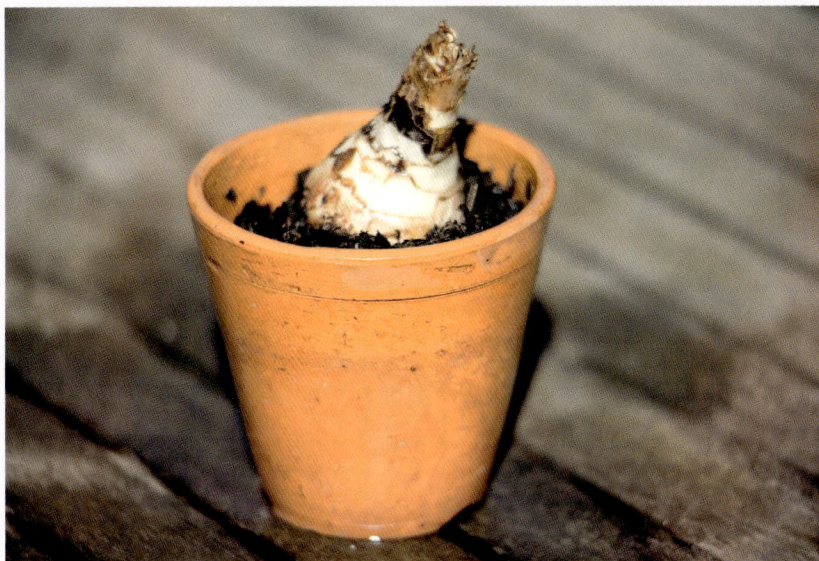

Above: Once potted bulbs have finished flowering, feed them and remove them to a spot protected from rodents, to be brought out again next year.

5 October

The tea roses

It is about now that the first rose blooms in my Sydney garden. It is my favourite rose, a climbing tea, *Rosa* 'Marie van Houtte', whose blooms are the colour of clotted cream, with a light splash of crushed raspberry. Her elegant buds take a few days to open into a blowsy, but not too relaxed, full bloom. She is planted with a honeysuckle that flowers in crushed-berry colours: one that does not become rampant.

A national collection of tea roses has been established at the Araluen Botanic Garden, Perth, to ensure their continuing survival and to provide a study resource. Many largely evergreen and constantly blooming varieties, with their heritage in the warmer southern provinces of China, and which love the West Australian climate, provide a succession of colour through much of the year. Garden stars include the soft-pink 'Mrs BR Cant', the pink, very fragrant 'Mme Antoine Mari', the cerise 'Papa Gontier', the salmon pink to gold 'Mme Berkeley', the rich-yellow double-bloomed 'Isabella Sprunt' and the cream 'William R Smith'. There are beds devoted to roses bred by Alister

Above: The rose 'Sunny South'
Previous pages: At Fran Rawling's garden, Wylde Willow, at Dunedin, on New Zealand's South Island, the roses are at their magnificent best in late spring.

Clark, including the deep-red, fragrant 'Restless', the apricot-pink 'Mrs Fred Danks' and the golden 'Lady Huntingfield', 'Sunlit' and 'Marjorie Palmer'. There is also a hedge of the golden-bloomed remontant 'Sunny South'.

6 October

Mown grass paths

If you are lucky enough to own a garden large enough to necessitate the use of a ride-on mower, you can also use the mower as a design tool. With its help, you can create softly sweeping paths through a meadow, and mark out garden areas.

7 October

Clivias

There is no plant more prepared to cooperate in dry shade than the clivia, which will be starting to bloom in many parts of the country. The genus was named, in October 1828, by the botanist John Lindley, after Lady Charlotte-Florentia Clive, Duchess of Northumberland and granddaughter of the famous Clive of India. The plant was thriving in the duchess's greenhouse, having been earlier introduced to England from South Africa by the botanist James Bowie, a staff member of the Royal Botanic Gardens at Kew.

The popular orange-flowered *Clivia miniata* looks smart planted en masse and lighting up the dark shade under evergreen trees. Clivias flower best when kept dry, so they are perfect for planting in pots, under eaves, where they won't catch too much rain. In recent years, the coveted cream- and apricot-flowering varieties, along with the vibrant red—once the domain of collectors only—have become more accessible for gardeners in Australia. Be alert for the clivia caterpillar, however, which can devastate a plant over- night. Combat in the evening with the non-toxic (to humans) Dipel, or, spray with Baythroid.

The clivia caterpillar can also devastate belladonna lilies.

8 October

Sir Hans Heysen

The artist Sir Hans Heysen—nine times winner of the Wynne Prize for landscape painting—died on this day in 1968. Heysen's work is put into per- spective by a visit to his house, The Cedars, and his beloved garden, in their setting of eucalypts, at Hahndorf in the Barossa Valley.

There is a large collection of roses throughout the garden, some planted in enormous beds of the perennials that Heysen loved to paint. At the bottom of the garden is a glade dominated by a very old crab-apple (*Malus spectabilis*), and, beyond, another rose garden that includes the artist's favourite, 'Souvenir de la Malmaison'. The entire garden is bordered with Heysen's beloved river red gums (*Eucalyptus camaldulensis*) and white gums (*E. rubida*). The majestic river red gum is a key motif in Australian iconography, often depicted by painters against shimmering summer heat, and providing shade for resting cattle.

9 October

Orchids and moving water: refreshing and cooling!

Orchid festivals

The Hills District Orchid Festival (www.hillsdistrictorchids.com) is held four times each year at Northmead, in New South Wales. The organiser, David Banks, specialises in coelogynes, along with several genera of Australian orchids. The spring show is held over the second weekend of October. Nearby, the Galston District Garden Club holds its open gardens event on the third weekend in October each year. Ten gardens around the area—some on acreages, but some small—are open. Over the past decade $250 000 has been raised during the weekends and distributed to charities.

10 October

Companion planting

Companion planting, the method of growing certain plants together for their mutual benefit, has long been practised by vegetable gardeners. Certain combinations of species are thought to assist in warding off pests, preventing diseases, attracting bees for pollination, enhancing flavours, improving growth and fixing nitrogen. Most gardeners plant basil where they grow tomatoes; less well known companions are nasturtiums and apples, chamomile and cabbages, and dill or sage and brassicas. Parsley planted with tomatoes, asparagus and sweetcorn is said to improve their flavour. I am not sure that any of this works, but many of the combinations are charming to look at.

11 October

A hint of summer

While the mountain areas around the country are still thinking about spring, in the warmer regions, the promise of summer is in the air. A new selection of garden stars is getting ready to show off. The overlapping of the two seasons results in the happy collision of wisteria and roses. The few last, long racemes of the pink wisteria over my almost-white lych gate hang on, the scented pea-flowers blending with the first blooms of a climbing tea rose, the blush-pink 'Devoniensis'. You may also see the first gardenia of the season around now. The most common is *Gardenia jasminoides* (until recently *G. augusta*) along with its popular varieties 'Florida' and the large-bloomed 'Professor Pucci'. Who could forget their gorgeous scent? You want to bury your nose in the bloom, again and again: it is almost impossible to say 'enough'. They love rich, but well-drained, acid soil, and humid, frost-free conditions. As they are shallow-rooted, they are content in pots.

12 October

Coathanger hedges!

The function of hedges is not just to hide or divide: I love them when they are used as coathangers, encouraging climbers to scramble through their

The can-can colours of bougainvillea brighten up any garden.

foliage. Trees and shrubs with lemon-toned leaves—such as silver birch or mock orange (*Murraya paniculata*)—look effective with climbing roses such as the yellow Banksian rose (*Rosa banksiae* 'Lutea'), as well as *R.* 'Souvenir de Mme Leonie Viennot' and 'Paul's Lemon Pillar'. The richly scented murraya blossom also tones perfectly with white star jasmine, which can be planted beneath the hedge, to clamber up, filling in sections that have become sparse. And Banksian roses also look particularly effective if allowed to romp through a severely clipped, deep-green conifer hedge. The leaves of camellias are a good foil for the glorious trumpet vine (*Mandevilla* spp.), which flowers in a range of pinks and reds. Or, throw down a few packets of nasturtium seeds and allow them to scramble through a hedge at whim. I also love the companionship of a cerise bougainvillea—particularly the small-growing 'Bambino' varieties—flowering with a bright-pink oleander.

13 October

Two-spotted mite

Two-spotted mite, previously called red spider mite, is the bane of azalea, camellia, rhododendron and viburnum lovers. This pest causes leaf discolouration, and appears as small dots clinging to cobwebbing on stems and the undersides of leaves. As the plants finish flowering, spray with Confidor. (In colder climates you can do this in early November.) Follow up with a spray once each month during summer, ensuring that you spray the undersides of the leaves. PestOil and eco-oil will also work.

14 October

In temperate climates, wisterias will be filling gardens with scent. In colder climates, the first of the *Wisteria floribunda* will be unfurling. Nurseries around the country will have stocked up on 'potted colour': add advanced tubs of flowering petunias to terracotta pots for an instant fix of colour and scent.

15 October

Sculpture by the sea

Don't miss the annual 'Sculpture by the Sea' exhibition (www.sculptureby thesea.com) if you are anywhere near Bondi, in New South Wales, this month. The show, so emblematic of Sydney, with its references to water, and to the coastline, runs over ten days at the end of October, and into early November, each year. Visitors walk from Tamarama Beach to Bondi Beach, past rock formations, coastal caves and crashing sea, all providing the canvas for an eclectic collection of sculptures, large and small.

16 October

Flourless orange cake

This flourless cake, based on an ancient Sephardic recipe, has been a favourite with many friends, over several decades. Many cooks add their own minor variations which subtly change the texture and flavour; in our house, we increase the quantity of almonds, and my daughter Olivia adds several spices to the water in which the oranges are boiled. The cake freezes well.

Orange and almond cake

3 medium oranges, whole, unpeeled and scrubbed
1 clove
1 cardamom pod, crushed
1 quill cinnamon
6 eggs, beaten
250 g caster sugar
200 g ground almonds
50 g blanched whole almonds, coarsely ground
1 teaspoon baking powder
icing sugar, to dust

Put whole oranges, and spices, in a saucepan, in water to cover, and bring to the boil. Simmer for 1 hour, topping up the water when necessary. Drain, and discard spices. Allow oranges to cool, cut into eighths, and discard pips. Chop roughly in food processor.

Pre-heat oven to 180°C. Line and grease a 24-centimetre springform tin. Beat together eggs and sugar in a bowl, then add almonds and baking powder. Fold oranges through the mixture. Pour into the tin. Bake for 1 hour, or until a skewer inserted into the centre comes out clean. Allow cake to cool slightly, and then turn out onto a wire rack to cool further. Dust with icing sugar and serve, warm, with thick yoghurt.

Succulents save water in Nancy Brewer's Ballarat garden.

17 October

Water-wise euphorbias

It's time to consider the list of plants that make up your garden. Is it full of thirsty, fragile prima donnas, or easy-going and water-wise species, plants that will survive the hot days that all parts of this country experience in late spring and summer—in some regions for days at a time? Why not buy some xerophytic plants like succulents? They store water from good seasons, to be used in times of drought. The group includes aeoniums, agaves and aloes, bromeliads and cactuses, echeverias, euphorbias, and sedums and sempervivums.

Euphorbias—considered too commonplace by some gardeners—are tough, hardy and not too thirsty: summer saviours. Among several new varieties is the compact *Euphorbia* 'Ascot Rainbow', which has green to grey and cream foliage that turns pink to burgundy in winter. *E.* 'Black Bird', with its deep-cerise foliage, teams wonderfully with purple-leaved cannas and with edgings of black mondo grass. *E.* 'Emerald Empress', which reaches

50 centimetres and bears forest-green foliage, looks great with a hot-pink salvia. *E.* 'Craigieburn', which forms a compact shrub, and *E. myrsinites* and *E. rigida*, which will tumble over a low wall, or down a bank, illuminate the winter garden with their lime-green foliage. But take care: euphorbias, members of the poisonous Apocynaceae family, exude a milky sap that can irritate skin and eyes.

The sedums, including *Sedum spectabile* 'Autumn Joy' and *S. matrona*, are also invaluable in a water-wise garden. Other plants that will thrive without much water include the Australian native sage (*Plectranthus argentatus*)— although this species can make itself a little too much at home, taking root wherever you leave a cutting. Honeybush (*Melianthus major*), with its soft, serrated foliage, bears spikes of brick-red flowers, followed, during winter, by indigo berries, and is water-wise and greatly loved by birds. As it is native to South Africa, it is not surprising that it can be invasive in warm climates. The New Zealand rock lily (*Arthropodium cirrhatum*), with its grey leaves and spires of white flowers, tolerates dry shade and looks good all year. The feathery, fragile-looking foliage of sacred bamboo (*Nandina domestica*) belies its hardiness, and the native correas are tough, thriving in shade or sun, if given perfect drainage. Gardeners in frost-free climates find fountain, or coral, bush (*Russelia juncea*) a saviour, as it will thrive on neglect: with the slightest amount of care it bears red funnel flowers from pendulous chandeliers of foliage—great for covering a bank, or to cascade over a retaining wall.

The succulent bed in Ballarat's botanic gardens shows that these tough and water-wise plants make a perfect companion for roses: it includes an *Echeveria* 'Black Prince' and *Aeonium* 'Velvet' in front of a black *A. arboreum* 'Schwartzkopf'.

18 October

Garden art

During the last week in October, the Friends of Sydney's Royal Botanic Gardens hold their annual 'Artisans in the Gardens', an exhibition of superb craft and art with a horticultural theme. The works include statues and fountains for the garden, ceramics, textiles and jewellery. Entry is free and all the displayed works are for sale.

19 October

Creeping fig

The creeping fig (*Ficus pumila*) looks great covering a brick wall. Be alert, however: it must be kept well clipped to ensure that the foliage remains small, with fine, juvenile leaves. Never allow the vine to fruit, or you will find it becomes strong enough, and aggressive enough, to enter, and damage, the point work. The creeping winterberry (*Euonymus fortunei*) also looks wonderful clothing a wall.

20 October

Sydney Opera House

The Sydney Opera House was opened on this day in 1973, by Queen Elizabeth II. Standing on Bennelong Point, where the First Fleet landed in 1788, the Opera House is overlooked by the Sydney Botanic Gardens. Flowering now in the gardens is the most spectacular king orchid (*Dendrobium speciosum*) that you are ever likely to encounter.

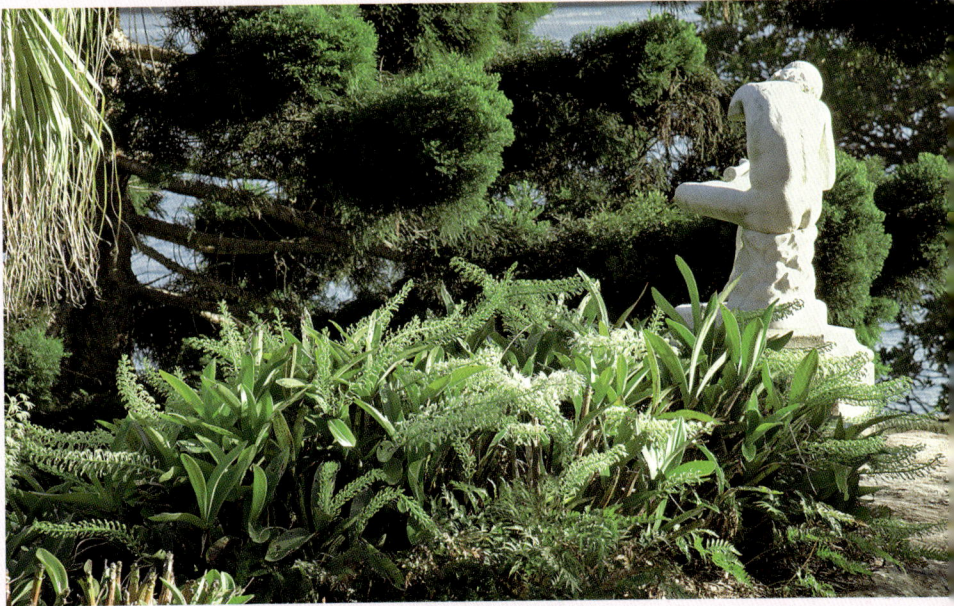

The glorious native **king orchid (*Dendrobium speciosum*)** blooms each October.

21 October

Salvias

The Roman scientist and historian Pliny the Elder named the hard-working and easy-going salvias. There are almost 1000 species and varieties of *Salvia officinalis*, flowering in all colours from pale pink, magenta and red, to blue, lilac and yellow. Most salvias have tubular flowers, held high on square stalks. The foliage varies in texture from smooth to velvety, and in colour from deep green and olive, to red-tinged and grey; some have scented leaves, among which it is always pleasant to work. Salvias occur naturally in most parts of the world, so, whatever climate you garden in, there will be a salvia to suit. They will be muscling up now; in fact, in some regions they make themselves a little too much at home—they are, after all, members of the mint family. Some are invasive, such as bog sage (*S. uliginosa*), which is a problem in good soils, but you may find them to be a godsend if you garden in conditions where many other plants struggle, such as on the coast.

Among the best salvias for humid and coastal climates are varieties of the *microphylla* species, including the hot-pink 'Margaret Arnold'. Blue-flowered salvias include the beautiful *S. azurea*, *S. patens* and *S. chamae-dryoides* (which likes cooler and drier conditions); these are easy to grow and propagate. Plants from the *greggii* species are recommended for less humid climates, south to Melbourne, and for dry inland gardens. Among the larger flowered cultivars are *S. guaranitica* 'Costa Rica Blue' and 'Black and Blue', which nevertheless don't reach a metre in height, making them suitable for smaller gardens. Cut them back after the first flush of flowers to ensure an autumn showing.

22 October

Nancy Steen Memorial Garden

The Nancy Steen Memorial Garden opened in 1984, dedicated to the New Zealand rosarian born in 1898, and part of Auckland's Parnell Rose Garden. It will be at its flamboyant best from now, through November. Nancy Steen dedicated her life to preserving the old roses that she collected from cemeteries in which the earliest of New Zealand's European settlers are buried, and from roadsides. Her book *The Charm of Old Roses* is a lively description of her lifelong quest to find and preserve these roses; in it she depicts the flowers as intimate friends, and details their idiosyncrasies, their faults and their virtues.

The luscious 'Nancy Steen' rose

The memorial garden is a quarter-hectare rectangle into which several long rectangular beds are set. Two sturdy pergolas add height to one end of the White Garden and are covered in *Rosa* 'Wedding Day', the popular climber bred in the United Kingdom by crossing two Chinese species, *R. longicuspis* and *R. moyesii*. Steen also adored *R. dupontii*, which she called 'The Snow Bush'. This vigorous climber, loved for its trusses of white blossom and its elegant apple-green leaves, was bred by André Dupont, director of Paris's Luxembourg Gardens.

In the White Garden, the glorious climbing tea rose 'Mrs Herbert Stevens', prized for her long buds, is accompanied by the white form of 'Cecile Brunner', and 'Anna-Maria de Montville', a charming sprawling rose bred in the south of France in the nineteenth century. Shrub roses add another layer of structure and intrigue, including the delicate 1832 damask 'Mme Hardy', which flowers throughout summer with its distinctive green 'eye' at the centre of white, cupped, scented blooms.

The long beds that skirt the garden are packed with perennials and roses, all flourishing behind low hedges of box. The sunset colours of R. 'Mutabilis' crowd around the edges, restraining the pink-flowering 'Bloomfield Abundance' and the glorious carmine 'Mme Isaac Pereire', with her voluptuous scent. Tall foxgloves and larkspurs flower among the roses. Another bed runs the length of the garden and houses a collection of early-flowering tea roses, including the 1878 'General Schablikine', flowering orange and pink. Coming as they do from southern China, the old tea roses cope well with the humid conditions of this harbourside garden.

Even if you are not devoted exclusively to old roses, a visit to this lovely garden will leave you, in Steen's words, 'charmed with their beauty'.

23 October

If you can get your hands on spoiled lucerne, use it to create a water-saving, weed-repelling mulch for your garden.

24 October

2, 4, 6, 8

Every Australian country woman grew up with this recipe as a standby: it is a basic cake batter recipe, to which any number of variations can be made. It can be used as a batter to bake on top of any fruit in season; spices can be added, or nuts, or chocolate. It can be spread into a slice tin, cut into slices and sandwiched with cream and jam, or served hot as a tea cake. It has been enjoyed at morning smoko in country kitchens and shearing sheds, served with morning coffee at the tennis mornings that have long been part of country life, and contributed to community fetes.

Two, four, six, eight cake

The name of the cake lingers from the days of imperial measurements.

2 eggs
4 oz (125 g) butter
6 oz (180 g) sugar
8 oz (250 g) flour
milk

Grease a 22-centimetre springform tin. Preheat oven to 180°C. Mix eggs, butter, sugar and flour together, and add enough milk to bind. Mix in your own variations, then bake for 45 minutes, or until a skewer inserted into the centre comes out clean.

25 October

Mulch it!

The first of the hot days will have hit by now, so it's time to ensure that your weeding, feeding and, most importantly, heavy mulching are all done, ready for high summer, when the heat will arrive regularly. You can choose from a variety of mulches, from spoiled lucerne, to composted woodchip, to coir, sugar cane and cotton trash. Coco mulch can be purchased in blocks at nurseries. Inexpensive mulching materials might be local to where you live. For instance, one country gardener I know lives near an essential oils distillery and obtains, free of charge, quantities of 'herb trash', which makes an excellent water-conserving ground cover. If you live near a winery, you might have easy access to inexpensive grape marc. Rice husks, which decompose slowly, make an excellent mulch and soil conditioner. Take care if using woodchip, as it uses nitrogen as it breaks down; ensure that it is well aged before application. The best mulch of all is your own home-made compost, which is also a wonderful fertiliser.

26 October

Jacaranda blooms an intense blue along with the cerise to purple blooms of a bougainvillea.

The ultimate entrance

It's time for end-of-year exams in most states around Australia. This means the jacarandas will be flowering, on bare stems, in their unique shade of blue. When the winter has been dry, the colour seems even more intense. The fast-growing trees often unwittingly play host to bougainvilleas, a stunning combination. Native to Brazil, they enjoy dry winters and hot summers.

In 1890, the main street of Grafton, in New South Wales, was planted with sixty jacaranda trees. The Grafton Jacaranda Festival (www.jacarandafestival

.org.au) was the first flower festival to be held in Australia, in 1935. It is still held, over several days in October, with the last Thursday of the month dubbed 'Jacaranda Day': the town goes mad with the lilac theme, hosting parades and the crowning of a jacaranda queen.

More jacarandas can be seen a few hours' drive south of Grafton, close to Port Macquarie: the driveway leading into Cassegrain Winery is lined with jacarandas, Illawarra flame trees (*Brachychiton acerifolius*) and silky oaks (*Grevillea robusta*). With the brilliant-red blossom of the flame tree held against the blue of the jacaranda and the umber inflorescences of the silky oak, the sight is a traffic stopper.

27 October

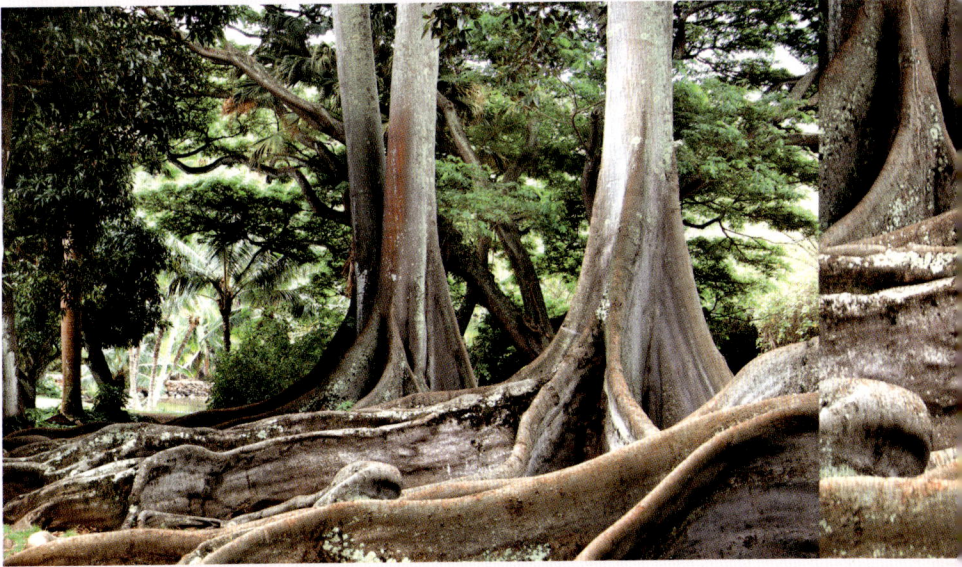

These Moreton Bay figs, thriving at Allerton Gardens, Kauai, have featured in several Hollywood films.

Fabulous figs

James Cook, the British naval captain and explorer, was born on this day in 1728, in Yorkshire in the north of England. During the course of his travels he is believed to have transported seed of the Moreton Bay fig tree (*Ficus macrophylla*) from Sydney, where it occurs naturally, to Hawaii. The large fast-growing fig, which reaches some 30 metres along the warm temperate parts of the east coast of Australia, was popular for parkland planting during the nineteenth century. The species is distinguished by its aggressive roots, which extend out, across the ground, as somewhat prehistoric-looking buttresses.

28 October

Brideshead Revisited

Evelyn Waugh was born on this day in 1903. The television adaptation of his laconic novel *Brideshead Revisited* (which created a new generation of boys called Sebastian) was filmed, in 1981, and again in 2008, at Castle Howard, in England's north. The house has been home to the Howard family since 1701, when Charles, third Earl of Carlisle, engaged the architect Sir John Vanbrugh to create for him a suitable country seat. In 1772, Horace Walpole described Castle Howard as 'the noblest lawn in the world fenced by half the horizon … I have seen gigantic palaces before, but never a sublime one'.

The white climbing rose 'Wedding Day'

Among the garden treats, all set within a heroic landscape, is the rose garden, created on the site of an early eighteenth-century walled vegetable garden. The structures that support the various roses are particularly intriguing, and different methods of pruning also provide many lessons for visitors. Some bushes are opened out like an inverted tent and tied to bamboo stakes. Elsewhere, several bushes of a single cultivar or variety are pruned high on woven supports to form a sort of elevated groundcover. The rose garden is divided into 'rooms' by hedges of yew or pleached beech (*Fagus sylvatica*), with arches in them leading the visitor from one section to the next. The central walk passes a stone-edged pond, around which are four wedge-shaped beds, edged in box, and filled with the David Austin rose 'Chianti', again, pruned to form a high groundcover. Tripods of sweet peas add height to the various beds in this symmetrical design. Along one side of the rose garden is a pergola 42 metres long and covered in the perfumed white rose 'Rambling Rector', again, clipped to encourage the buds to mass up and cover the entire pergola, which is underplanted with rare old-fashioned roses like the gallicas 'Alexandre Laquement' and 'Berenice', and with the Bourbon 'Souvenir de Mme Auguste Charles'. This is backed with a brick wall covered with 'Mary Washington' and with the modern yellow rambler 'Ghislaine de Féligonde'. One section of the wall is clothed in the climbing *Hydrangea petiolaris*.

Wrapping around the formal central sections are wide grass paths lined with borders of hostas, peonies, prostrate clematis (*Clematis integrifolia*), lavenders and dianthus. The North Yorkshire answer to the Mediterranean olive, the weeping silver pear (*Pyrus salicifolia* 'Pendula'), is planted in muted counterpoint to the intense greens in which this garden is painted.

29 October

The 28-spotted ladybird

There are over 100 different varieties of ladybirds in Australia. Sometimes called ladybugs or ladybeetles, most are, of course, beneficial to the garden, feasting on all sorts of pests, including scale and aphids. There is one species that none of us wants in our garden, however: she is the orange-coloured 28-spotted ladybird. She loves the leaves of vegies such as potatoes and eggplants, and will skeletonise the foliage, preventing photosynthesis and devastating the plant. She oozes a noxious liquid from the joints of her rear legs as a deterrent to predators. To combat her, pick her off your plants, and then feed them up to encourage health and vigour.

30 October

Don't waste walls: Chinese star jasmine clothes this vertical plane in Venice.

Vertical planting

Climbers satisfy the greediest of gardeners. Growing on vertical planes, spreading across supports, and clambering through hedges, they take advantage of every centimetre of the garden. Among the best is the Chinese star jasmine (*Trachelospermum jasminoides*), which will be covered tantalisingly at the moment, in frost-free climates, in buds. While some gardeners criticise it as *ordinaire* and in the north of the country admonish that it can become a little rampant, there can be no more useful, and beautiful, climber than this easy-to-please scented beauty. Whether trained on wires on an unattractive fence, or on a wall that might also support the seasonal growth of Boston ivy (*Parthenocissus tricuspidata*), used as a ground cover, cascading from pots or clambering up the bare legs of a hedge that has become a little sparse at its base, this climber is a trouble-free joy. In a restricted palette of mostly green plants, it can be part of a cool, soothing low-maintenance garden. It looks particularly lovely when soft-pink roses are allowed to romp through it. And when it is not in flower this jasmine forms a dense, green, lush-looking curtain, a perfect backdrop for the next garden soloist. Cut it back hard after flowering, and, during the high-growth period of summer, prune it to keep it tidy and to the desired shape and framework. Then, wait until late spring for the next scented treat.

31 October

Singapore trees

As Singapore has a great deal of lightning each year, more than 120 trees in the country's botanic gardens are protected with lightning conductors. There are many botanical stars in the gardens, including a range of exotic trees. The monkey-pot tree (*Lecythis ollaria*), a relative of the brazil nut, develops huge urn-shaped fruits; in the gardens it plays host to a selection of ferns that grow naturally in the forks of its branches. The cannonball tree (*Couroupita guianensis*) bears flowers on long stems that wrap around the trunk; the blooms, sweetly scented and ranging in colour from apricot to pink, are reminiscent of giant quince blossom. The fruits are not edible.

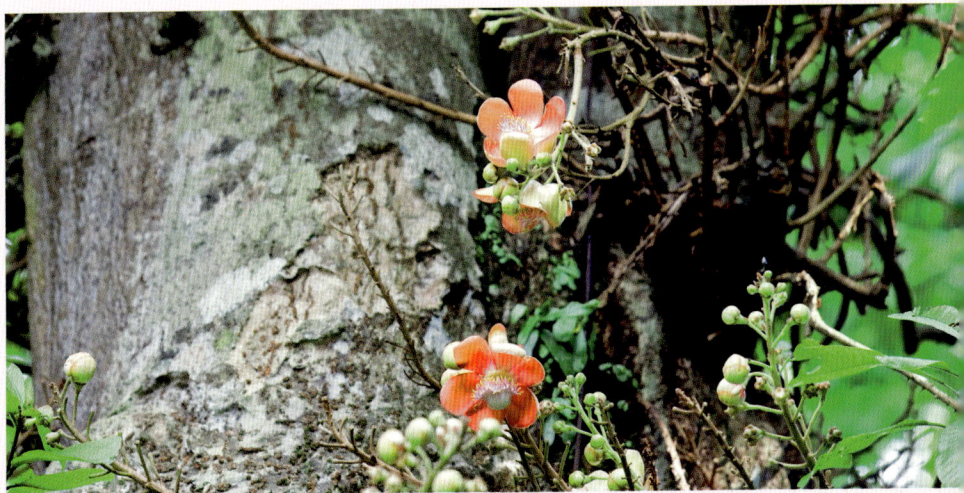

The fascinating cannonball tree, in Singapore Botanic Gardens, bears sweetly scented apricot-pink blooms.

November

1 November

Mount Tomah Botanic Garden

The ceiling of Rome's Sistine Chapel, painted by Michelangelo, was exhibited to the public for the first time on this day in 1512. The ceiling, 20 metres above the floor of the chapel, includes nine scenes from the book of Genesis, including the expulsion of Adam and Eve from the Garden of Eden, which is often said to have been located at the source of the four rivers that formed the cradle of civilisation: the Pishon, Gihon, Tigris and Euphrates. Almost five centuries later, the glorious Mount Tomah Botanic Garden, located in the Blue Mountains of New South Wales, was opened to the public on this day in 1987. Collections from cooler regions of the world thrive in the deep basalt soil, low temperatures and high rainfall of Mount Tomah, the 3-hectare cool-climate site attached to Sydney's Royal Botanic Gardens.

The gardens at Mount Tomah include a herb garden, divided into six beds filled with phlomis, rosemary, lavender, geranium and different types of stachys, and an adjacent rose garden, which features beautifully designed arches covered in wisteria and climbing roses. Entry to a lawn terrace is between two dogwoods (*Cornus kousa*) that guard an arch of blue-and-white wisteria. Australian conifers (*Callitris rhomboidea*) enclose this lawn, which is planted with the cool-climate perennial rye and chewings fescue grasses. The beds are edged with variegated thymes. Arches of yellow double Banksian roses direct the visitor up stone steps to an herbaceous border, where plants move from white at the centre, through tones of a single colour, to reds and oranges at the edges. A large pergola completes the garden. The entire area is backed with a massive hedge of rhododendron and set against an imposing backdrop of brown barrel (*Eucalyptus fastigata*).

2 November

High-altitude rhododendrons

In all the mountain areas around the country, rhododendrons will be at their peak. Prune rhododendrons little and often, by picking the blooms as they finish, rather than subjecting the plants to a severe cutting back every few years.

Blackheath Rhododendron Festival (www.rhodofestival.com.au) is held annually at Bacchante Gardens in the Blue Mountains, from mid October for a month, with a gala over the first weekend in November. There are wonderful walks across the 18-hectare site, through fern-covered valleys and around lakes, where mass plantings of azaleas and rhododendrons, along with beautiful exotic trees, have been introduced to blend with the bushland setting of native flora.

The vireya *Rhododendron commonae*, beside the pristine waters of Lake Piunde, 3200 metres up Mount Wilhelm in the central highlands of Papua New Guinea

3 November

Date with Melbourne Cup

Melbourne Cup Day occurs on the first Tuesday of November. It signals the day on which many gardeners plant their tomatoes and re-pot their begonias. (Although Tasmanian gardeners should protect their tomatoes, each night, against frost, until after Christmas Day.) Plant tomato seedlings quite deep, to encourage good root development. It is important to stake the taller varieties, such as 'Grosse Lisse', right from planting time. As they grow, continue to tie them up to strong wooden stakes. Pinch out the lower leaves to encourage growth at the top and to keep them reaching for the sky. You can train cherry and climbing tomatoes on netting, or on teepees and frames.

The late spring harvest ...

4 November

Walcha gardens

The New England area of New South Wales, now enjoying spring, is a region of inspirational cold-climate gardens. The Walcha Garden Festival is held over the second or third weekend in November, every second year, when eight of the district's best gardens are open. Among the gardens that have featured in previous festivals is Langleigh, where hardy perennials snow-in-summer and convolvulus cascade down retaining walls. Owner Robyn Cameron's discipline in choosing a restricted palette of hardy species has been very successful here; the result has been a quick and glamorous ground-cover. Plantings of catmint, iris, penstemon and lavender are each 3 metres in diameter and are backed with a tapestry of smoke bush, berberis, may, viburnum and lilac, all protected by dense conifer hedges. Throughout the surrounding paddocks are groups of trees, protected from the cattle by care-fully constructed tree guards. There are English elm (*Ulmus procera*), pin oak (*Quercus palustris*) and tulip trees (*Liriodendron tulipifera*). Along a bound-ary road there are copses of poplars (*Populus nigra* 'Italica'), which colour wonderfully in autumn. There are also golden elms (*Ulmus procera* 'Louis van Houtte') planted just outside the house fence to link the outside with the golden elm planted in the garden.

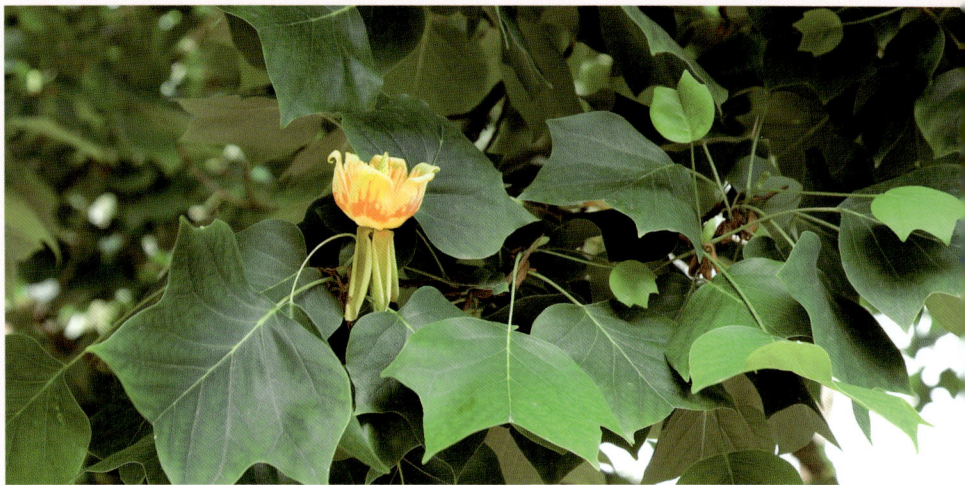

The golden blooms of the tulip tree in November. In autumn, the leaves turn butter-yellow.

5 November

Macadamias

Macadamia nuts—bauple nuts, enjoyed by Australia's Indigenous people for thousands of years—take me back to my childhood in Queensland, where many neighbours had the trees. Fingers were often bruised as we took to the protective brown shells with a brick, eager to get to the sweet, creamy-white kernel inside.

A study completed in 2008 by Southern Cross University's Centre for Regional Climate Change Studies demonstrated that macadamia trees play an important role in removing carbon from the atmosphere: the researchers found that 1 hectare of the trees is able to store 4 tonnes of carbon dioxide each year. The macadamia belongs to the Proteaceae family, and is a genus containing nine species of evergreen plants, seven of which are native to Australia. The explorer Alan Cunningham was the first European to find the plant, at Gilston in the Gold Coast hinterland, in 1828, but it wasn't named until 1857, by the botanist Ferdinand von Mueller, after his colleague John Macadam. The first tree taken from the forest was planted in Brisbane's botanic gardens in 1858.

Macadamia trees require warm, frost-free climates, and are self-pollinating. The white to pink flowers are produced in slender, simple racemes of about 20 centimetres in length, in winter and spring, and are followed by the nuts, which drop when mature, from late summer to autumn. A particularly attractive species is *Macadamia integrifolia*, which thrives north from Coffs Harbour, and grows to around 15 metres in height; it has glossy, smooth-edged, oblong leaves arranged in whorls of three.

6 November

Recycling week

It's pretty confronting to realise that more rubbish is produced in Australia per person than in any other nation except the United States—about 1 tonne each per year. But over three-quarters of the waste we produce is recyclable. Planet Ark's National Recycling Week is held each year during the second week in November, and aims to raise awareness about the importance of recycling, and to give tips to ensure our efforts are trouble-free. There is very little that cannot be recycled, and most food waste can go safely back to the soil in the form of your own homemade compost. As well, you can use newspaper (the sections without coloured inks) as a first layer of weed suppressant, or mulch; cut-off plastic milk bottles can become mini-greenhouses, or can house snail deterrents that cannot be accessed by pets. Unwanted CDs can be hung in fruit trees to scare off birds and possums, and netting from bought fruit can be wrapped around the fruit hanging on your own trees to provide protection.

7 November

Lavender

The square stems on your lavender mean that it belongs to the same family as mint; if only it were as easy to grow! Lavender will be preparing to flower now. Happiest in climates of hot, dry summers and cool, moist winters, this genus makes the perfect accompaniment for roses. It won't thrive in humid climates; think of Mediterranean regions, and the poor, rocky, alkaline soils of the south of France, with which lavender is synonymous.

The clever parterre of lavender blooms in early summer at Jack's Ridge.

English lavender (*Lavandula angustifolia*) is the best known and most common species, flowering from early summer. It is from the oil glands at the base of the flowers of this species, and of the French lavender *L. stoechas*, that lavender oil is distilled. Among several cultivated varieties of the *angustifolia* species is the much-loved 'Hidcote'. It was found by the American Lawrence Johnston in the hills in the south of France and taken back as seed to his garden at Hidcote Manor, in England's Cotswolds, and, along with 'Munstead' and 'Twickel Purple', is favoured for drying, while *L. angustifolia* 'Egerton Blue' is valued for its oil. Grow the later-flowering *L. angustifolia* 'Rosea' and 'Folgate' to extend the flowering season. If you adore lavender, but garden in a humid climate, you will enjoy greater success with the tough French lavender *L. dentata*, which performs through winter.

For success with lavender, sweeten acidic soil with an application of lime, and ensure the plants enjoy full sun and good drainage. Prune lavender every few months to prolong the life of the plant—but take care not to remove developing flowers.

8 November

The art of espalier

Think vertical: if your garden is small, why not espalier your choice of tree, whether you are growing citrus, stone fruit, or ornamental species? Espaliering is the art of pruning a plant to grow flush with a vertical surface, along a framework, usually of wires. It is not difficult to train most species, even giants like *Magnolia grandiflora*—which, allowed to grow naturally, would be too large for most suburban gardens—into fan shapes, rope-like cordons, or diamonds, which will quickly decorate any surface. It is the small-space gardener's answer to the sin of wanting it all. And growing fruit as espaliers on a warm brick wall will increase their yield; the trees are easier to care for, and more economical to harvest, and more trees will fit in the area used. Figs, apples and pears happily comply with this method of training, and even the elegant crab-apple is suitable for pruning in this way. Olives, risky planted as a tree in a small space, as the roots can run rampant, are kept in check when trained against warm walls.

9 November

Fertilise for growth

Make it a habit to fertilise your growing vegies with a soluble fertiliser in a watering can each fortnight. While plastic cans may not be as smart as the metal ones, I find them the easiest to use, as they don't clog up, or rust.

10 November

The decorative fence

There is almost no limit to the uses for fences and walls in a garden. They can frame views, divide space and direct attention in a certain way. They can also provide privacy, or vertical growing space. Or, they can simply be beautiful, a piece of garden art, like the Japanese tea whisk fence. Named for the whisk used in traditional tea ceremonies, the wall is created from reeds, prunings or twigs tied with cord, bamboo or wisteria into bundles.

Beautiful, and useful—the tea whisk fence in a Japanese garden

11 November

Black spot

Watch for the first signs of fungal problems and black spot on your roses, and spray with an organic fungicide: mix 3 teaspoons of bicarbonate of soda and 2.5 teaspoons of PestOil in 4.5 litres of water. Spray, over all foliage and stems, two or three times over a fortnight, and when the plant is clear, spray weekly.

12 November

Beetroot

Beetroot, which happily grows all year round, is a much-underestimated vegetable. It is full of nutrients, particularly vitamin B, high in fibre and low in fat, and is delicious prepared in a variety of ways. One of the best is to simply bake the washed beetroot; then remove the skin (using thin plastic gloves to prevent staining your hands). Chop into cubes, toss with crumbled goat's cheese, and serve on a bed of baby spinach, or lettuce leaves. For added pizzazz, add the juice of a couple of oranges to the roasting pan.

Hanging globes of white chrysanthemum daisies are easy to create.

13 November

Use an oasis

You don't have to be an experienced florist to create wonderful decorations with flowers, foliage, nuts and pine cones. You might consider making floral hanging globes to create an elegant look for a wedding, or other special event, at home. It's easy with florist's oasis and a few handy hints. Here's how: buy foam oasis, in globe shapes, from your florist, or from the suppliers you will find at your wholesale flower market. (Don't try to economise by re-using an old oasis, which will be full of bacteria that will reduce the life of your arrangement.) Before you add your decorative material, allow the oasis to float in deep water: never push the oasis into the water as bubbles will form, creating dry spots in the foam. Remove the oasis from the water and place it on a protected surface to create your arrangement. Cover the oasis with white daisy chrysanthemums: cut the stems to just 1 centimetre and push them into the oasis. Add a white ribbon and hang several (at varying heights) from a verandah or pergola. Take hanging arrangements down each evening to spray with water to keep fresh.

Tenjuan

Nanzen-ji Temple was built, in the foothills of the mountains to the east of the ancient Japanese capital, Kyoto, as a retirement villa for Emperor Kameyama, becoming a Zen temple upon his death, in 1291. Tenjuan, one in a series of sub-temples attached to the main building, is a simple, refined construction that overlooks an exquisite dry garden, which illustrates the aesthetic of Japanese landscaping of the late fourteenth century. Rock compositions, invoking ideals of longevity, can be viewed from the peace of the side verandah, a mediating space between the building and the garden. This is an introspective, meditative, intimate garden, which uses meticulously clipped shrubs and beautifully raked gravel beds to evoke a sense of a wider landscape.

The restrained elegance of Tenjuan, a sub-temple attached to Nanzen-ji, Kyoto

15 November

Delicious shortbread

This delicious shortbread can be cooked in a slice tin and cut into fingers. Or, drop teaspoonfuls of the mixture onto a tray and flatten with a fork; once cooked, join the shortbreads together in pairs, with icing. You can also use it as the base for a delicious strawberry shortcake. Simply bake the shortbread, allow it to cool and add strawberries and whipped vanilla cream for a perfect ending to a winter meal. And keep a quantity in the freezer for a pudding when you are 'caught short'.

Macadamia nut shortbread

2 cups plain flour, sifted with pinch salt
⅓ cup cornflour, sifted
½ cup icing sugar
250 g unsalted butter
1 cup raw macadamia nuts, roughly chopped
1 teaspoon vanilla essence

Preheat oven to 180°C. Mix all ingredients in an electric mixer. Spread onto a very lightly greased scone tray. Cook for 10–15 minutes, or until a light golden colour. (The shortbread will still be soft to the touch and will firm up when cool.) Remove from oven and cut into fingers while warm.

16 November

Botanical art exhibition

The exquisite work of many of Australia's best botanical artists can be seen at Sydney's Royal Botanic Gardens, in a biennial exhibition, held in November, showcasing species found in the three gardens run by the Botanic Gardens Trust. Among the paintings is that of an orchid developed from two den-drobiums that are native to Papua New Guinea, *Dendrobium engae* and *D. shiraishii*. This lovely plant blooms in two shades of green, with deep-purple stripes and rows of spots.

17 November

Native frangipani

If you've noticed a marvellous scent while on your morning walk, it may be the native frangipani (*Hymenosporum flavum*), which fills gardens—even in the cooler regions—with fragrance, and will be covered now in tiny white-

and-yellow blooms. The blueberry ash (*Elaeocarpus reticulatus*) and the tree waratah (*Alloxylon flammeum*), along with the Illawarra flame tree (*Brachychiton acerifolius*) and the silky oak (*Grevillea robusta*)—blooming with its umber, toothbrush-like inflorescences—are all at their best at this time of the year.

The native frangipani fills the garden with its scent in late spring and summer.

18 November

Decorative gardens

What is a potager? What sets it apart from a simple, workmanlike vegetable garden? Carefully designed with the decorative, as well as the productive, in mind, the potager is, perhaps, the ultimate in the design aesthetic: beautiful and useful. In the potager of my dreams I would install a wire fence, dug deep into the ground to deter rabbits and other pests. It would support—depending upon the climate—a series of vines, from soft fruits to passionfruit. My potager would be a square or rectangle divided by gravel or ant bed or decoratively laid brick paths (mown grass being too difficult to keep looking good in this situation). These would separate slightly raised beds edged in palings of plantation-grown hardwood—strong and wide enough for me to sit on when I want a break from weeding, and on which I could rest the tea tray.

I have a friend in Ballarat whose smart potager thrives under a regime of crop rotation, soil improvement, clever watering and frost protection. Four triangular, wood-edged beds house, and rotate, brassicas, including the

Oh, for a vegie garden like this! Ballymaloe Cooking School, Shanagarry, in the south of Ireland.

decorative and delicious black kale, potatoes and root vegetables, including carrots, beetroots and parsnips, and leaf vegetables, including beans and leeks. Rocket and nasturtium are squeezed into any bed, so that they can be picked at all times to spice up a salad. 'Green Dragon' broccoli is also grown all year. One bed is left fallow each season.

19 November

Old-fashioned roses

The once-a-year old-fashioned roses will be preparing for their annual performance. Among the most important of the old roses are the gallicas, developed from the wild *Rosa gallica*. In turn, they have contributed to the classes we call the damasks, albas, centifolias and moss roses. The oldest cultivated form of *R. gallica* is 'Officinalis', or the 'Apothecaries' rose', well known through its use as a symbol of England's War of the Roses. It is thought to have first appeared in the French town of Provins, where it was used in perfume production and for medicinal purposes. It bears deep-pink semi-double blooms, which have a rich fragrance. One of the loveliest of the gallicas, 'Duchesse de Buccleugh', was bred in France in 1846.

The damask rose is thought to have been taken to France from Persia (modern-day Iran) by the returning Crusaders. Among the important cultivated varieties is 'Ispahan', which appeared before 1832, and flowers for weeks in early spring with voluptuous rich-pink, wonderfully scented blooms. The ancient 'Kazanlik', also known as *R. damascena trigintipetala*, is one of the species grown at Kazanlik, in Bulgaria, for the production of attar of roses. 'Omar Khayyam' was bred in about 1893, supposedly from a seed gathered from the rose on the poet's grave at Nashipur, in Iran, also the town of his birth.

And the once-flowering climbing rose 'Albertine' is so thorny that it is wise to plant her where she can grow uninhibited, and where she doesn't need to be pruned: romping up a deciduous tree, perhaps, that needs little attention. Any of the deep-pink clematis—such as the large-flowered burgundy 'Niobe'—team wonderfully with the single-flowered 'Mme Gregoire', ensuring that your interest is held for weeks.

Watch out for the tiny holes in unopened rose buds that provide evidence of budworm: once they get inside the bud, sprays won't kill them. Spray early with Confidor, Dipel or Success.

At Badine, the garden of Kathie and Arthur Mills at Orange, New South Wales, the rose 'Mme Gregoire Staechelin' flowers each November.

20 November

Iron chelates

All members of the Proteaceae family—which includes banksias, grevilleas and waratahs—benefit from an application of iron chelates during the warmer months. Iron in the soil helps plants to take up nutrients; a lack of iron in native plants causes yellowing leaves and stunted growth.

Ballarat District Garden Festival

The Ballarat District Gardens in Spring festival is held in late November, and is an opportunity to wander in city and country gardens that are thriving in the midst of drought. A diverse range of designs, from large country properties to outstanding examples of city gardens in compact spaces, take part.

There are exceptional town gardens, such as Nancy Brewer's, which demonstrates stylish innovations and clever adaptations to cope with severe water restrictions. Some of the gardens rely on native plants, and others are full of exotics. The garden at the historic Old Curiosity Shop reveals the timeless quality of the cottage garden, and the Ballarat Community Garden displays sustainable productive gardening with ideas to incorporate into home gardens. Jan Todd's resplendent vegetable garden is packed with survival ideas and whimsical garden sculpture created from old farm tools. Among the country properties often open, landscaper Elizabeth Gilfillin's elegant garden is arranged around the gentle whites and creams of scented viburnums and old-fashioned camellias: if you are lucky, her magnificent wisteria will be blooming still. At another country garden, The Laurels, at Learmonth, 10 kilometres from Ballarat, several of the trees are listed on the National Trust Register of Significant Trees: they were planted by the first owner, William Vaughan, who arrived on the Victorian goldfields from Hereford, England, in 1852.

Climbing roses

If space is limited in your garden, you may concentrate on climbing roses to dress vertical structures such as walls and fences. They will be looking fabulous now in cool climates. Yellow roses like 'Alchymist' and 'Yellow Charles Austin' are wonderful teamed with wisteria—but this is not a combination to employ if you prefer a low-maintenance garden. To encourage the greatest flowering from climbers, tie the stems down flat—as horizontal as possible—to promote stress, and shoots, all the way along the branch.

Flowering only once each year, the flamboyant, but thorny, 'Albertine'

23 November

Tricks with mirrors

It is fun to experiment with mirrors in the garden. Clever placement of mirrors can make a small space appear much larger, and can create a sense of mystery and intrigue in small, or large, gardens. A well-placed mirror, perhaps to reflect a door, will create the illusion of several more garden areas beyond. Or, add a rustic wire bed frame, that you might have picked up in a recycling shop, to a plain mirror, for added artistic effect. Remember, though, to consider what will be reflected: will it create a pleasing effect? You may want to experiment with an inexpensive piece of mirror before you invest in a quality, long-lasting mirror.

24 November

Sweet carrot treat

Among the most delicious of sweet treats is the carrot cake, and you can almost convince yourself that it is good for you: as well as all the carrot, this rich, moist cake is packed with dried fruit and walnuts. Un-iced, the cake freezes well. It also works with zucchini instead of carrot.

Carrot cake

FOR THE CAKE

500 g carrots, grated or processed

½ cup caster sugar

1 cup light olive oil

2 cups self-raising flour,
   sifted with pinch salt

2 teaspoons spices
   (I like ginger, cinnamon and nutmeg)

1 cup each walnuts and raisins

FOR THE TOPPING

½ cup icing sugar

250 g cream cheese or ricotta

2 tablespoons sour cream or crème fraîche

1 teaspoon vanilla essence

Preheat oven to 180°C. Lightly grease a 22-centimetre springform tin and line the base with baking paper. Mix all cake ingredients, in the order given above, in an electric mixer, finishing by folding in the raisins and nuts with a wooden spoon. Cook for 1 hour, or until a skewer inserted into the middle of the cake comes out clean. For the topping, mix ingredients together, and spread over the cake once it is cool.

25 November

Alliums

Alliums, summer-flowering bulbs planted earlier in the year, before the weather cooled, will be flowering now, with their spectacular globe-shaped heads, comprising hundreds of tiny violet star-like blooms. With inflorescences held on stems up to 60 centimetres long, they add gravitas to any cool-climate border. They won't perform in humid regions, however, so, if you want their razzamatazz, but live in a warm temperate climate, grow onions or garlic instead, and allow some to develop flower heads before harvesting.

26 November

Green Harvest

Fruit exclusion bags are the latest innovation from Green Harvest (www
.greenharvest.com.au), the horticultural company helping to keep us organic.
The delicate bags can be tied around individual fruits to keep out flies and
moths; they are no deterrent, however, to possums or bats, but the company
offers a range of other exclusion bags that should keep out bigger pests.

27 November

The garden of May Gibbs

Contrary to common belief, perhaps, Nutcote, the garden of children's writer
May Gibbs, was not full of the native plants that peopled her books. She
ventured into the bush to source her characters, including the banksia that
inspired the 'big bad banksia men' and the 'gumnut babies', Snugglepot and
Cuddlepie. Her harbourside garden in Sydney was actually replete with
roses. May Gibbs died on this day in 1969, aged ninety-two.

28 November

Peonies

If you garden in a cold climate you have probably indulged in those luscious
beauties peonies (*Paeonia* spp.), which will be putting on their flamboyant
performance about now. It is easy to understand the attraction of the peony.
Cultivated in China for centuries, featuring in literature and gracing porce-
lain, paintings, textiles and lacquer work, the peony expresses delicacy and
strength at the same time. The ethereal blooms represent elegance, purity and
breeding. The healing powers of the peony were detailed by Pliny the Elder,
the leading Roman authority on science during the first century AD, and it
is thought they were introduced to England by the Romans.

There are more than thirty species of deciduous perennials and
shrubs in the genus—mostly from Asia, although a few are indigenous to
North America—and thousands of named cultivated varieties. They bloom

in colours ranging from scarlet, cerise and pale pink, to cream, white, yellow and even almost black. Flowers can be single to very double, described by breeders as anemone, crown-type or bomb-type, often with ruffled petals. Most peonies need a cold winter, during which the herbaceous species die back to the ground to initiate the flower buds; this is the time to add a rich manure and mulch, and then watch in wonder as fat red shoots unfurl as the frosts clear and long stems develop rose-like flowers by the end of spring. The Chinese tree peony (*Paeonia delavayi, P. suffruticosa* and *P. lutea*, among others) is more likely to grow successfully in the temperate to warm climates in Australia; it has woody stems up to 3 metres in height and produces enormous, flamboyant, usually double, heads each spring.

Peonies dislike being moved, so choose their spot in the garden carefully; but if you must move them, now is the time. Cut them back, lift and replant, watering in and mulching well.

Luscious, lovely. Peonies are heavy feeders and dislike humid climates.

Gertrude Jekyll

Gertrude Jekyll was born on this day in 1843, in Mayfair, London, the fifth of seven children. She became one of the most influential garden designers and writers, not only of her time, but for all gardeners. Skilled also in embroidery, woodwork, silversmithing and photography, Jekyll (her name rhymes with treacle) was central to the Arts and Crafts movement. A chance meeting, in May 1889, with the twenty-year-old architect Edwin Lutyens, led to a collaboration that resulted in over 400 houses and gardens, commissions that relied upon strong lines overlaid with exuberant planting schemes. A prolific writer, Jekyll contributed over 1000 articles to home and garden magazines, and published a dozen books, the first of which, *Wood and Garden*, was released in 1899.

The roof of Australia

The walk to the top of Mount Kosciuszko, at 2228 metres Australia's highest peak, and much safer in the warmer months of the year, is among the greatest of experiences for those who seek out special places. Visitors climb, or take the chair, to the top of the main range above Thredbo village in the Snowy Mountains, and from there follow a well-marked trail to the summit. Much of the trek is on a wooden boardwalk, to protect the fields of wildflowers that bloom during summer above the tree line, from about 1850 metres.

Among the first of the tiny native species to flower in spring are the marsh marigolds, which push through the rocky soil as soon as enough light penetrates the melting snows. The purple-and-white eye bright blooms until Christmas, and is followed by billy buttons, silver snow daisies and alpine celery until the end of January. The gentle meadows of the high country flower between brutal granite outcrops and imposing bare, rocky peaks which rise around pristine, clear alpine lakes.

As you gaze across the folds of the silent mountains, shimmering blue with their cover of eucalypt, to Dead Horse Gap and on, into Victoria, you might reflect upon the way in which the quiet spiritualism of this place is addictive: it will ensure that you return again.

December

Pot up plants for Christmas presents now

1 December

Christmas presents

Along with baking the Christmas cake and preparing the plum pudding, the time has come, again, to think about Christmas presents. Was that a groan I heard? If so, you are not alone in experiencing a sinking feeling when faced with the high expectations that seem to accompany the festive season. Why not revisit the idea of making your Christmas presents? The garden can offer plenty of ideas for personal gifts: preserved lemons, pots of flowering hydrangeas, a pretty fruiting chilli in a small tin bucket, a basket of vine-ripened tomatoes, or pictures made from pressed flowers. A jar of slow-baked tomatoes, roasted for up to four hours in the lowest oven possible, cooled and packed in good-quality Australian olive oil, is a wonderful accompaniment for Christmas seafood. A herb garden, in a smart—or simple—pot, also makes a great gift, and will keep on giving over many months. Take a shallow pot filled with the best potting mix available, and pack it with a combination of tall- and low-growing herbs: borage, for the bees, at the rear, a staked small-growing tomato plant, a good-size tub of basil, and smaller pots of coriander, sage, trailing thyme and nasturtium.

2 December

Saving water

Many Australian cities are often under severe water restrictions. Artist and gardener Nancy Brewer, from Ballarat, uses a range of clever techniques to ensure that no drop of water is wasted. She cuts back anything she can during hot weather, to reduce transpiration, and deadheads continually to keep the garden looking fresh. Most of her plants are drought-tolerant, and she constantly edits to remove thirsty species. Mulch is essential, of course, and is always applied to damp soil that has been watered with Seasol and a tablespoon of dishwashing detergent (to assist in the uptake of moisture) added to a bucket of water.

Crucial to the garden's survival is the collection of water. Any downpipes that are not directed into household water tanks are diverted outside. A bucket is kept under the overflow from the hot water service, and bowls in sinks catch rinse water. Washing machine and shower water is channelled onto the garden. It goes without saying that all cooking water can be cooled and tipped onto the garden or onto pot plants. Nancy also collects any container that can be adapted to deliver moisture. For example, large plastic containers of mineral water that are fitted with a tap are refilled with collected water after use, and deliver water in a slow drip to shrubs and fruit trees.

3 December

Gardens for everyone

Today is the International Day of People with a Disability. There are many ways in which the home garden can be adapted for, and enjoyed by, someone with a disability. For example, consider the height of garden beds: raised beds, built to waist height, mean that plants can be tended more easily. Wide edges on garden beds will provide a place to sit, to work in the beds or simply to contemplate the garden. Wide, even paths allow for safe wheelchair access. Sensory gardens, full of textured and scented species, can be chosen for the enjoyment of those who have a vision impairment. With a little thought and planning the therapy and sense of companionship to be enjoyed through gardening are available to all.

Edna Walling

Edna Margaret Walling was born in Yorkshire, England, on this day in 1895. She became one of Australia's foremost garden designers, graduating from the School of Horticulture at Burnley, in Melbourne, in 1918, and paving the way for women to succeed in this previously male profession. Her beautiful gardens, many of which remain extant, more than fifty years after they were constructed, and the exquisite watercolour plans she created, have ensured that her work remains influential into the twenty-first century. The scaled-up dry-stone walls that often formed the backbone to her gardens—and were usually constructed by Eric Hammond, her preferred stonemason—along with her understanding of the essential balance between planted spaces and voids, contributed to the success of her designs.

The stone wall at Markdale, on the Southern Tablelands of New South Wales, was built by Eric Hammond, Edna Walling's favourite stonemason. It remains extant today.

Christmas bush

The New South Wales Christmas bush (*Ceratopetalum gummiferum*) will be appearing in the markets now, reminding us that Christmas will soon be here. Among the best varieties is 'Albery's Red', which grows to some 5 metres high and 2 metres wide. Native to the coastal areas of the state, the plant demands well-drained soil.

6 December

Friends of Botanic Gardens

A great Christmas present for people who enjoy gardening is membership of the friends association of a local botanic garden (www.friendsbotanicgardens .org). Along with the capital cities, many provincial towns throughout Australia have created public gardens of botanical importance, and they each have a friends association. Members work to encourage the advancement of horticulture and botany, scientific research, education and, most importantly, friendship.

7 December

Prunes

If you adore plums, you'll probably love prunes, too. The prune is, of course, a dehydrated plum, most often from the French 'Agen' variety. Most prunes are produced in California, and it takes 3 kilograms of fresh plums to produce 1 kilogram of prunes, which are high in fibre. Prunes are delicious wrapped in bacon and grilled, when they are known as 'devils on horseback'. Or, prick them with a fork, soak them in liqueur, and serve with good vanilla ice cream and hot homemade chocolate sauce for an utterly decadent pudding.

8 December

William Guilfoyle

The landscape gardener William Robert Guilfoyle was born on this day in 1840. Generally acknowledged as the designer of Melbourne's Royal Botanic Gardens, of which he was the director, from 1873 to 1909, he also created many public and private gardens throughout Victoria. Guilfoyle was the eldest son in a horticultural family that arrived in Sydney in 1853. After opening a nursery at Redfern, his father, Michael, was commissioned to landscape Greenoaks, the Darling Point property of the merchant Thomas Mort. Guilfoyle senior then opened a much-admired nursery on 3.5 acres in Double Bay, and was involved in the landscaping of Sydney's Botanic Gardens and the Domain.

William Guilfoyle was pioneering the sugar cane industry in northern New South Wales when he was invited to become curator of the Melbourne gardens. He nursed a grand vision for their design, assisted by the wealth of the city at the time: Melbourne was entering its golden period and there were few financial restrictions on Guilfoyle's vision and genius. The sweeping Romantic landscapes of eighteenth-century English masters William Kent, 'Capability' Brown and Humphry Repton were most influential on Guilfoyle, although he created his landscapes on a more intimate scale and favoured an element of surprise in his plans. His plant-hunting expeditions to the Pacific islands are also reflected in the gardens: in the fern gully, for example, the eighteenth-century Romantic landscape is overlaid with the nineteenth-century 'Paradise Style'.

9 December

Bomana War Cemetery, Port Moresby

10 December

Make cut flowers last

Make your cut flowers last longer with these few simple tips. When you pick, or purchase, flowers, snip the ends of the stalks before you place them in water. And strip off the leaves that will remain below the water level; leaves above the water should remain in place. Pick flowers in the cool of the early morning, or in the late afternoon. And change vase water at least every second day, snipping stems each time. Rinse out vases with bleach after use. When picking roses in bud, cut off a little of the stem and place the roses in tepid water, in a cool place, for a few hours before arranging. This prevents the buds from opening too soon.

11 December

National Rose Garden

Rose gardens in colder areas will be in full bloom, including the National Rose Garden (www.woolmers.com.au), set in the historic Woolmers Estate, close to Launceston in Tasmania. Opened in 2001, this 3-hectare garden takes visitors on a journey through the history of the rose. The entrance, beyond the outbuildings and homestead of the Woolmers Estate, is through an 80-metre arbour of the German-bred climbing rose 'Westerland', its orange-and-apricot blooms tying the garden to the ochre-washed buildings behind.

The rose 'Westerland'

12 December

Squeeze those lemons

Prune summer-fruiting trees after the fruit has finished. Then, feed, water well and mulch. At this time of the year, lemons can be thick-skinned and somewhat tough, and difficult to juice. Put them in the microwave for 30 seconds to make juicing easier.

13 December

The Wollemi pine

It's almost time to put up the Christmas tree, and, instead of an exotic pine, or the chopped-off top of a radiata pine, you may perhaps consider our new-found fossil, the Wollemi pine (*Wollemi nobilis*). After Christmas keep it in a pot to ensure that it does not grow to anywhere near the 30-odd metres that it reaches in its natural environment, in the warm temperate forests of the mid-north-east of New South Wales.

14 December

Cicada song

When the cicadas reach their full-throated chorus, they just sing of summer! Some of the common names for the different species of cicadas are most attractive: there are 'Floury Bakers' and 'Double Drummers', along with 'Greengrocers', or 'Yellow Mondays'. Cicadas don't contribute anything to the garden, except to provide food for birds and insects. I am not sure that they do much damage, despite the fact that they pierce plants and suck their sap. Their main feature, apart from their interesting form and markings, is their marvellous melody!

15 December

Sweet potato

The sweet potato (*Ipomoea batatas*) is not actually related to the potato, but is a member of the same family as morning glory: Convolvulaceae. The Spanish word for sweet potato is *batata*, its similarity to the English word potato explaining, perhaps, the confusion.

16 December

Vases

Any receptacle that will hold water can be used as a vase. So, a little lateral thinking can lead to teapots holding roses; watering cans bearing stems of fruit trees, perhaps with fruit still attached; and charming old glass bottles containing bunches of herbs. I have even seen gardening boots holding posies of pansies.

Vases: limited only by your imagination.

17 December

Frangipani

The tough but beautiful frangipani (*Plumeria* spp.), the prehistoric-looking member of the poisonous Apocynaceae family, will be coming into bloom, conjuring up images of carefree summer days. The genus has just eight species, mostly deciduous and native to Central America. The trees can reach up to 14 metres in height; the fragrant salver-form flowers, from 5 to 13 centimetres in diameter, appear in early summer at the end of somewhat bizarre tortured-looking, rubbery branches, and before the leathery, deeply veined mid-green leaves appear. There are thousands of varieties, most derived from *P. rubra*. The easiest to grow, and probably most common in this country, is the

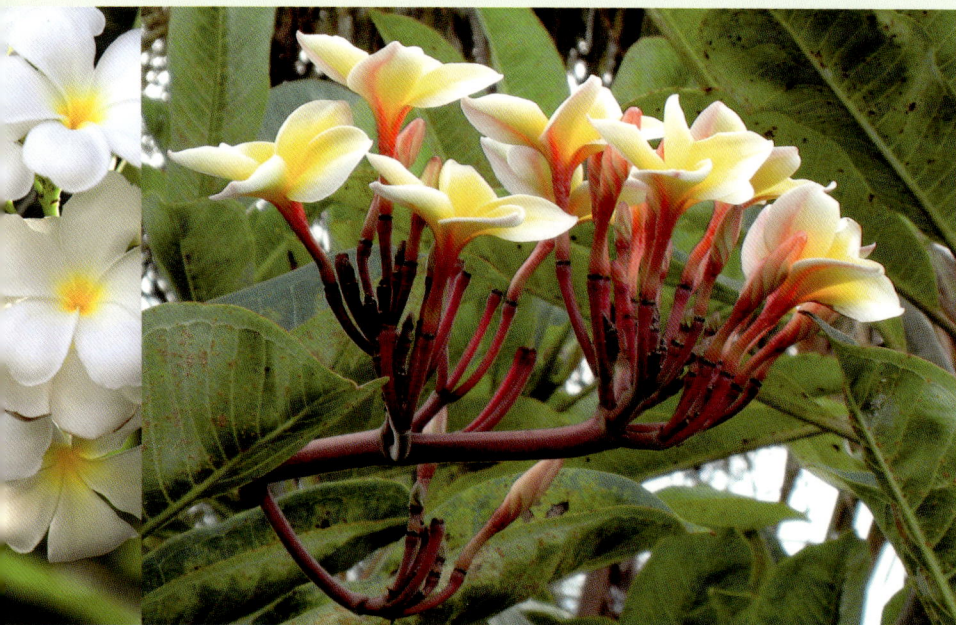

Frangipanis: left, the evergreen *Plumeria obtusa*; right, *P.* 'Molilii Gold'

yellow-and-white *P. rubra* var. *acutifolia*. The *P. rosea* has gorgeous orange to yellow centres to the flowers, which range from pink to carmine at the edges, and evoke dreams of tropical sunsets. *P. rubra* f. *rubra* bears crimson flowers on a broad canopy, while *P.* 'Peach Glow Shell' blooms in fruit salad colours.

Frangipanis can be successfully employed in many ways, in gardens large and small. They make wonderful features for courtyard gardens, creating shade in summer, but welcoming light and warmth when bare in winter. In Hawaii, frangipanis are planted in avenues, bending artistically over double hedges: often clipped hibiscus teamed with a lower hedge of foliage plants such as crotons, or even bromeliads. The dwarf cultivars are suited for growing in containers in cool temperate climates, where they must be taken inside for winter protection; many other varieties will thrive outdoors all year round, as far south as Sydney. All frangipanis are undemanding, requiring only a frost-free environment, well-drained soil and several hours of sun daily. In cooler climates, place frangipanis near a north-facing wall that will retain its warmth. Fertilise, after flowering, with a high-potassium product. Be careful of the white sap exuded from the stems, and flower bases: it is poisonous.

18 December

Versatile clematis

Clematis must be one of the most versatile and useful of plants. Traditionally used to cover a trellis or a pergola, or hide the unsightly 'bare' legs of climbing roses, the plants add excitement to a plain hedge or form an impressive ground cover. It is a genus somewhat underutilised in this country, however, perhaps because of its reputation for being difficult to grow well. Clematis is an enormous genus, from the Ranunculaceae family, and includes over 200 species and more than 1000 cultivars, most native to the Northern Hemisphere. Among the easiest to grow are many in the vigorous Montana group, which hails from the Himalayas, China and Tibet. Many are vanilla-scented. They bloom on the previous season's wood, so you need to prune as soon as you can bear to part with the fluffy seed heads that follow the late spring and summer flowers. Clematis love a limey soil, but I have found they also grow well in rich, acidic soils.

Clematis grow towards the sun, but like their feet in the shade. Keep their roots cool by cutting a square of shade cloth, with a hole in the centre, and an opening in one side to allow placement over the root area. Cover with mulch to disguise the cloth. When planting, dig a very large hole and add plenty of well-rotted compost. Plant with three sets of nodes under the ground, so that the plant will shoot strongly.

19 December

Summer says sunflowers

Summer sees sunflowers (*Helianthus annuus*) in full, sunny bloom. Loved by children and adults (including certain artists), these cheerful flowers, held on tall stems, bring golden light to balmy evenings. Named after Helios, the Greek god who travelled across the sky in the chariot of the sun, sunflowers turn their faces to the sun each day. The plant has been cultivated for centuries, but it is thought to be native to South America, where it grows naturally. A large selection of cultivars is available in Australia, providing blooms in red, orange and yellow, and in single, double and very voluptuous forms. 'Dwarf Sensation' is perfect for pots and small gardens.

Sunny sunflowers are a happy sight in summer.

20 December

Summer hollies

In Australia, we can't pick rich-red holly berries to decorate Christmas platters and puddings, but, as well as the gorgeous colours of the eucalypts and the hot pinks and purples of sweet peas, many shrubs bear brightly coloured berries during summer with which it is possible to adorn the house. Among the best is the holly-like coralberry (*Ardisia crenata*), the genus of which has some 250 species: evergreen shrubs that occur in many parts of the world, in all climates. From Japan, China and the Himalayas, the coralberry is happy in temperate climates; in this country it grows to about 2 metres and produces layered branches of glossy, deep-green foliage which bears star-like white flowers in spring, followed by red berries.

Gum trees will still be flowering, filling the markets with blossom to grace the Christmas table in a uniquely Australian way. Among them, the somewhat inappropriately named yellow gum (*Eucalyptus leucoxylon*) blooms in a mass of deep-pink hanging blossom. The 'Summer Series' eucalypts will also be flowering, in marvellously clashing pinks and reds, oranges and apricots: they look fabulous together in a large vase.

Warm temperate gardens will be filled with gardenias. If you garden in frosty climates, you may, perhaps, buy some to decorate your Christmas table: there is, surely, no more glorious a fragrance. The gorgeous can-can colours of the hard-working fuchsias can also add Christmas cheer to tables and mantelpieces.

21 December

Winifred West

Winifred West was born on this day in 1881, in the pretty English village of Frensham, in the county of Surrey. Frensham is a quintessential English village of stone houses set in beautiful gardens of burgeoning flower borders, and no doubt influenced the gardens that West created around the school she founded in 1913, also called Frensham, at Mittagong, in New South Wales. West's aesthetic and her assumption that beauty is superior to utilitarian concerns become apparent upon observing the magical, enchanting garden she created at the school. It is set in wide open spaces; terraces are supported by stone or brick walls over which English-style perennials fall freely. West's favourite flower, the iris, is the school symbol, as it grows strongly in difficult conditions; a single iris remains the only prize that students receive. The main lawn at the school, on which an original eucalypt remains, providing a shaded gathering place for students, is integral to the sense of peace that pervades this garden that was so important to West. Two weeks before she died, in 1971, aged eighty-nine, West was still gardening, digging with a full-size spade, transplanting and reshaping, and planning future gardens.

22 December

Summer solstice

The longest day of the year, the summer solstice, is when the sun is in its most southerly position. So, when the foliage has died down, it's time to harvest garlic: hang the bulbs in an airy position until you are ready to use them.

23 December

Bananas

Banana flowers are edible, and not just to the blue-faced honeyeater, also known as the banana bird. It's peak season for bananas, that nature-wrapped fruit that is high in fibre and rich in vitamins A, B6 and C, as well as in potassium. Bananas are essential to many cuisines, particularly in South-East Asia and the Indian subcontinent, where they are used to cool down hot curries. In Australia, it's possible to find somewhat exotic varieties, like 'Senorita', which has pale-orange flesh and thick skin, and 'Red Dacca', which has pale-pink flesh and an orange to red skin. 'Cavendish' is the most widely grown variety in this country, but I love the smaller 'Lady Finger', which is sweeter, and whose flesh doesn't seem to go brown when exposed to air. 'Blue Java', 'Ducasse' and 'Goldfinger' are also available. Most bananas are harvested when green and hung in an airy room to ripen: my father used to suspend them from a beam in the garage, and break off a couple at a time.

These days, a permit is required to grow bananas in Queensland, and in some areas of New South Wales, to protect the banana industry from diseases such as bunchy top virus, Panama disease and black sigatoka, a leaf spot fungal disease.

24 December

Christmas wreaths

Christmas wreaths traditionally welcome guests over the holiday period, or can add sparkle and glamour to the table. It's easy to make a fresh wreath, which will survive the holiday period if you make it close to Christmas Day. Buy a foam oasis and its container from your florist. Cut stems of camellia, magnolia, holly, bay, or even eucalyptus, and create a solid green background. A much quicker cover is achieved with moss, purchased from a florist or market. You simply stretch out the moss thinly over the oasis, and secure it with short 'hairpins' made from 20-gauge wire (also bought from the florist supplier). This forms a base to which you can add berries, small pine cones or bows that you have wired. Different looks can also be achieved by attaching bunches of sweet-smelling cypress or spruce to your base wreath. Perhaps add a perky red ribbon to finish it off. Spray the wreath with water each evening to keep it fresh.

25 December

Christmas Day

Christmas Day! And this is the only day of the year that the Ballarat Botanical Gardens are not open. Botanic gardens are the second most visited places in Australia. (The first is the movie theatre.) We have eight capital city botanic gardens, and many provincial towns throughout Australia have also created public gardens of botanical importance: some 150, in fact.

26 December

Well-clipped hydrangeas make a smart hedge and will flower through summer.

Happy hydrangeas

It's a day for tidying, and for topping up the water in the vases of Christmas floral displays. Hydrangeas will be flowering, with their mopheads or flat, lacy blooms, in a jewel box of colours. While most hydrangeas are once-only flowerers, a variety called 'Endless Summer', released in 2006, blooms repeatedly, with flush after flush of big panicles, in blue or white. Save all water—from cooking and rinsing dishes, as well as in buckets as the shower heats up—to throw on your hydrangeas, as they are particularly thirsty when blooming.

After cutting hydrangeas—in the cool of the morning, please—crush the stems slightly and plunge them immediately into water that you have waiting nearby. They also love having their heads dunked into water. Flowers of mophead hydrangeas (*Hydrangea macrophylla*) left on the bush will fade to wonderfully soft, antique colours.

27 December

Scent of Murraya

In warm and temperate climates, hedges of mock orange (*Murraya paniculata*) will be flowering, filling gardens with their heavenly citrus-blossom scent. In some climates—the sub-tropical north coast of New South Wales, for instance—the plant is considered a weed, although, as it is most often used clipped into an effective hedge, I have yet to observe it left to go to seed.

28 December

Simple summer pud

The simplicity of this recipe belies the fact that it is decadently delicious. It makes the most of wonderful fruit absolutely in season and adds the richness of whipped cream and vanilla. It is so easy, but so delicious.

White peach and grape gratin

6 white peaches or nectarines, sliced
½ kg seedless white grapes
400 ml cream, whipped with
   1 tablespoon icing sugar and
   1 teaspoon pure vanilla
several tablespoons brown sugar
1–2 tablespoons marsala (optional)

Arrange peaches on a shallow baking dish (that you will bring to the table to serve). Sprinkle with marsala, if using. Add grapes on top. Top thickly with cream. Sprinkle generously with sugar. Brown under the grill until sugar is bubbling. Chill in refrigerator for at least an hour. Serves eight.

29 December

Bay tree

Leaves of the bay tree (*Laurus nobilis*) can be picked, and tied into bunches, to hang in your pantry, where they are said to be useful in deterring that great nuisance the pantry moth. And, of course, the leaves are marvellous in many recipes, from bolognaise sauce to casserole, and they add a woody scent to potpourri. Or, add a small cutting of the freshest and softest of the leaves to a tussie mussie.

30 December

Tall trees

Ancient trees have a character all of their own. Witness to years of growth, with massive trunks often bearing wonderfully marked bark and holding outstretched branches, they are precious. Until 2008, a swamp gum (*Eucalyptus regnans*) in Tasmania's Styx Valley, 'Icarus Dream', standing at 97 metres and with a diameter of 4 metres, was thought to be the tallest known hardwood. Next to it stands another swamp gum, 'Triarius', which is 86.5 metres tall. However, in 2008, 'Centurion', a swamp gum of 101 metres, was discovered in state forest close to Hobart, and has claimed the title. Californian redwoods (*Sequoia sempervirens*), in cathedral-like forests on the east coast of North America, are the world's tallest softwoods.

31 December

New Year's resolutions

New Year's Eve: the time when good resolutions are made! Today is also a chance to reflect upon the joy your garden has brought you through the year, from the chemical-free vegetables you grew, to the scent of the blooms of spring. The exercise you gained as you dug, weeded and mulched surpasses what might be gained indoors, in the gym. The satisfaction of creating something beautiful, and the wonder of seeing the seasons turn full circle, are therapy, too. The serendipity of garden-making, as colours in the garden team, and contrast, beautifully, with no prior planning, never ceases to amaze. And the perfection of nature, which never seems to make a design faux pas, continues to delight.

Index

THE MIEGUNYAH PRESS

THIS BOOK WAS DESIGNED AND TYPESET BY PFISTERER + FREEMAN

THE TEXT WAS SET IN 10 POINT ADOBE GARAMOND PRO

WITH 5 POINTS OF LEADING

THE TEXT IS PRINTED ON 130 GSM MATT ART PAPER

THIS BOOK WAS COPYEDITED BY PENNY MANSLEY